W9-BAR-326

Chapter VIII

Chapter IX

Introduction

hy tassels? What is their function? Today, it's purely decorative if you live in the western culture, although there are definitely more functional tassels that serve as livestock identification, to denote the hierarchy of a tribal lineage, and to depict successes in battle primarily in Asia, South America, and Africa. There are also numerous ecclesiastical types of tassels that serve as basic ornamentation or signify holy times of the year and the church hierarchy.

This book focuses on tassels that are relevant to *us*, that we would like to use for our homes. When you travel or read or look at a magazine, look for the tassels. You will be surprised how often tassels and fringe are shown and how they affect our appreciation for ornamentation. Since tassels are functionally mostly superfluous, this also leaves open the door for experimentation in their creation.

The goal of this book is to introduce all creative people to the art of tassel and fringe making. I have endeavored to eliminate or simplify the time-consuming and difficult techniques of traditional tassel-making to increase the enjoyment factor in the actual creation of these wonderful statement projects. The "keeping it simple" philosophy is inherent in ultimate success, in my opinion. It is making projects that appear more complicated to make than they actually are, a kind of trompe d'oeil effect of which only you, the creator, are aware. Yet these are heirloom pieces still, since so much of the value of these tassels and fringe projects is in the materials you select as well as the composition of the design.

Since I am a firm believer in the abilities and creativity of each person, and would like to expose different styles of design to you, I include two friends in this book. The first, Suzann Thompson, is a published and accomplished sweater and polymer clay designer. Designing tassels is the most obvious combination of those two mediums. So meet Suzann and her fabulous tassels on page 118. Suzann shares the instructions for her Fantasy Flower tassel, for those of you with a bit of polymer clay experience. The second friend, Alma Gulsby, is not only a designer, but an inventor. It was through her invention, the E-Z Winder, that we met. We both had a similar idea for twisting and winding threads using a bobbin winder, but she put the idea into an actual product. This tool, described in Chapter III, is invaluable for very quick twisting of threads for making into bullion tassels and fringe. By introducing these creative women to you, I hope to encourage you to be your creative best.

Terrific Tassels & Fabulous Fringe is primarily a pattern and technique book, so I intentionally keep the prose to a minimum; there are so many other authors who cover the historic references to tassels. My purpose is to provide inspiration as well as information - inspiration from Scalamandré's Mark Goodman and from the designers/inventors for whom tassels are a passion and livelihood. So whenever you visit a hardware, housewares, yarn, craft, or fabric store, or whenever you look in your own stash of collected containers, buttons, trimmings, etc. - all those things you knew there had to be a use for - you will look at them from an entirely new perspective and say, "Ah! That would make the most fabulous tassel!"

Cari Clement

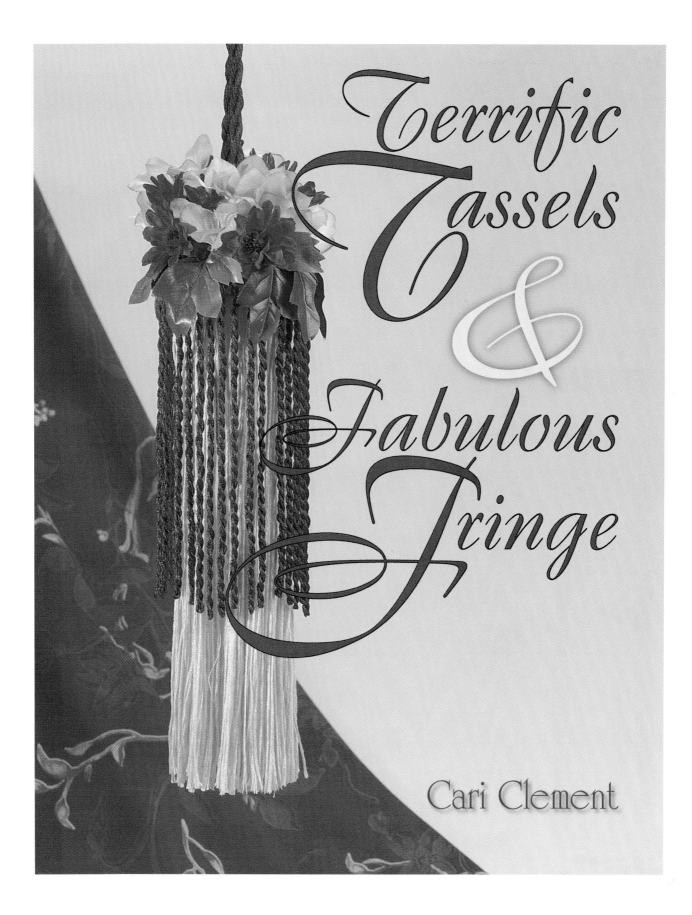

Terrific Tassels & Fabulous Fringe

Cari Clement

Published by

krause publications
700 E. State St.
Iola, WI 54990-0001
Telephone 715-445-2214
www.krause.com

Please call or write for our free catalog. Our toll-free number to place an order or obtain a free catalog is 800-258-0929 or please use our regular business telephone 715-445-2214 for editorial comment and further information.

Library of Congress Catalog Number: 00-102688

ISBN: 0-87341-819-0

Printed in the United States of America

The following companies or products appear in this book:
Black & Decker® WorkMate®, Boye/Wright's Crochet Fork, Cernit®, Clover Pompon Maker, Decowrap™, Extend-a-Tassel™, E-Z Twister™, E-Z Winder™, Fabri-Tac®, FIMO®, Incredible Sweater Machine®, Kreinik Blending Filament, Kreinik Custom Corder™, Leonardo Rope Maker™, Lustersheen®, Magicord® Machine, Multi's™ Embellishment Yarn, Peel 'n Stick™, Polarfleece™, Pom-Beadz™, Premo!™, Ribbon Floss™, Sculpey®, Spinster™, Steam-a-Seam® 2, Tassel Master™, Tassel Tops™, Tatool™, Trim Tool™, Ultrasuede™.

Dedication

This book is dedicated to my mother, June Bernice Mullon Clement, who made an obstreperous child into a creative woman through her unique ability for teaching the art of fiber manipulation: knitting.

Contents

Exceptional Applications
Using Tassels in Your Home

To get you on your way to making fabulous fringed accessories and tassels for yourself and your home, I've included this chapter to give you a visual connection to the use of fringe and tassels. Although when we think of tassels, we usually think of Victorian homes with graceful and occasionally fanciful accents, the tassels included in this book are not particularly Victorian. Rather, they are meant to appeal to a wide range of tastes.

Even if your living room happens to be in a style that may not lend itself to tassel and fringe ornamentation, the bedroom is a wonderful place for tassel accents. Even those of you with contemporary, seaside, country, or Asian decor will find tassel patterns in this book that would be appropriate in your homes.

"Statement" tassels not only lend a dramatic look to your home, but are also conversation starters. If your decor is based on a rustic theme, make tassels that use pine cones or decorative birch branches as their finials. If you have a seaside cottage, use seashells as finials. If you are an avid gardener, make tassels with finials (or skirts) made from dried flowers from your garden - or silk flowers from your local craft store. If you are planning a special look for your holiday decorating, tassels made in holiday colors can lend a truly memorable touch to your decor - especially as superlative tree ornaments.

The tassel and fringe applications in this Gilded Plum decor represent a reasonable yet multiple use of tassels and fringe. You can use the fabric, trim, yarn, and beads of your choice when you make the lampshade pictured. Accent the lamp with pillows, a fringed afghan, fringed and tasseled table scarves, accent tassels, a beaded tassel bookmark, bullion fringe on the chair, and a tasseled footstool. It all works together.

And then there are tassel and fringe embell-ishments on clothing. Historically, tassels have been used on clothing longer than in homes. Tassels defined the hierarchy of the Catholic church in the Renaissance period and earlier. They denoted nobility in ancient China. And they served the very practical purpose of holding down the head scarves of the Indigo people in Africa, whose clothing was constantly blown by the winds off the Sahara.

Today some of the most interesting uses of tassels are as pendants and earrings with metal chains for skirts. I also like the use of tassels as weights and have added them to the bottom of a very lightweight scarf with the hopes it no longer unwraps and flies down the street. Tassels on slippers denote a touch of class. Add a tassel to that special beret, use one as an identity mark on your purse or a surprise in your briefcase. Use a tassel to find your keys in the bottom of your purse. Put an accent on a dress pin and add it to your jacket. Add a soft, color-ful tassel to the handle of your luggage to easily spot it on the conveyor belt. (You'll not find some guy picking it up by mistake!) The applications are endless. Regardless of the style of décor you prefer, there is a fringe and tassel accent that will work perfectly.

This French Country setting makes use of tassels and fringe in a very different way. Don't toss out that favorite chair slipcover - embellish it with fringed chair "scarves." Accent a frame, add a table scarf, toss a pillow. Make it romantic and comfortable with the softness of fringe and statement of tassels.

For the look of luxe, add a dramatic tassel to an already rich velvet drapery accented with fringe. Just imagine how different this would look if you took away the fringe, tieback, and tassel.

And for that truly special day, why not use an elegant tassel added to a tulle bow on the ends of the pews? You could even use them as gifts for your wedding party! A bridal tassel lends a feeling of Victorian elegance to any wedding.

Embellishing plain purchased or hand-made stockings is a real treat. Create stockings in the favorite colors of the recipient, match colors and styles for a family group, or just use them to decorate the hearth.

For the holidays, tassels and fringe are everywhere. Be your creative best by adding your own tassel ideas. Since wire-wrapping is so popular, why not wrap a candle and hang on a few mini-tassels? Then tie it all together by accenting a table runner with a wire-wrapped tassel finial.

Chapter II

Inspiration & History
An Intimate Look at Scalamandré

A Historical Perspective

Scalamandré. The word alone denotes ultra *luxe*, elegance of a bygone era, elaborate trimmings suitable for a palace, a certain richesse. One visit to the Scalamandré showroom on Third Avenue in New York City will confirm that observation and then some. Their trimmings and tassels division, also referred to as *passamenaria*, caters to well-known interior designers and museums as well as to the upscale wholesale trade. The company will design any trimming or tassel to the client's specifications, however these services do not come without their price tag, which should be looked at as an investment.

San Francisco Plantation tassel created at Scalamandré.

A brief history of the company takes us from its origins in 1929 by Franco Scalamandré, a refugee from fascist Italy, to its current leaders, Robert F. and Mark J. Scalamandré Bitter, grandsons of the founder. Franco Scalamandré was a descendant of a long line of French and Spanish artisans who immigrated to southern Italy in the 1700s. Raised near the center of the silk industry in Italy, his move to textiles was a natural one. After a confrontation with Mussolini, Scalamandré was faced with imprisonment or exile.

Scalamandré's experience in America started at a shipyard and progressed to teaching architectural design at the Sealey School of Interior Design in New York. With design commissions originating from his work at the school, he was able to finance the opening of his own silk weaving company. When he married Flora Baranzelli, he had the ideal partner to expand his business and they worked together for many years - he handling primarily the operational side and she primarily the design side.

Luxe: The Scalamandré Showroom

I had the immense pleasure of a guided tour of Scalamandré's archival tassels and trims display by head designer and trimmings director, Edward Goodman, who ran Standard Trimmings before that company was purchased by Scalamandré. Goodman is not only one of the best tassel and trimmings designers, he is also immersed in the history of his trade. His background is the ideal (and rare) combination of economics and design, so not only do his tassel and trimmings designs have tremendous appeal to his clientele, but they are profitable for the company to produce as well.

Goodman travels the world for his inspiration, but Versailles, the summer home of Louis XIV and Marie Antoinette, has proved the most fruitful location. To underscore that, Goodman duplicated the Marie Antoinette tassel shown, one of the elaborate tassels from the Vanderbilt Mansion in Hyde Park, New York. The original design for this superlative tassel is believed to be from one commissioned by Marie Antoinette for Versailles. This tassel is so detailed and time-consuming to create, its price tag lists at a mere $9,000. However, not to be outdone by the Vanderbilts (or Marie Antoinette for that matter), one of Scalamandré's clients ordered a number of these tassels for her $250,000 bedroom makeover.

Marie Antoinette tassel.

In the Scalamandré showroom, Goodman showed me the historic tassels he has created for various rooms at the White House and other national historic buildings as well as antique tassels he's collected that are reminiscent of the antebellum period and earlier. The roster of historic homes and landmarks that use Scalamandré's services for the re-creation of textiles of all kinds including fabric, trimmings, fringes, and tassels, is far too extensive to list here, but includes over 900 historic projects. Some of the most notable are the White House, the Metropolitan Opera House, the Thomas Edison House, the Confederate White House, the Clara Barton House, and numerous state houses.

One of a set of tassels that is particularly interesting is pictured at right. This tassel is from the Old Merchant House. The bullion is quite dramatic and the ornamentation on the skirt and finial (called a "mold" by Scalamandré and others in the trimmings trade) complements the skirt perfectly.

Tassel from the Old Merchant House.

The exhibit also includes a striking blue and gold tassel that was created for the temporary White House and one from the drawing room of the White House of the Confederacy. Then there are the Vanderbilt tassels commissioned for their Breakers house in Newport, designed for their 80-room "cottage." Some tassels were designed and constructed in France, then imported. Goodman's reputation in the industry has afforded him very special consideration, so when historic tassels go on the market, he is notified so he may add to his exceptional collection.

The documentation and historic (and often memorable) references to trimmings either created or duplicated by Scalamandré are some of the more interesting notations to historic events and people:

❧ The color scheme in the White House Blue Room was originally thought to be a pale French Blue, which is the color Jackie Kennedy used. When Hillary Clinton learned that the correct color was a much richer Empire Blue, she changed it from the one Jackie Kennedy had installed.

❧ The fringe on the flag decorating Abraham Lincoln's booth the night he attended the fateful performance at the Ford Theater in Washington, D.C., nearly foiled John Wilkes Booth's escape when, in fleeing the scene, he caught his heel in the fringe. Scalamandré used some of the original fibers from this flag in reproducing it for the theater.

✾ After a visit to Monticello, Franco Scalamandré was convinced that the historic accuracy of the décor was lacking. Since Jefferson was such a world traveler, Scalamandré felt the sparse and delicate nature of the window curtains belied their true origins, since silk damask was the sought-after fashion in Europe at that time. After much research, Scalamandré discovered Jefferson's original drawings for his home, which did include damask draperies. Needless to say, Scalamandré handled the reproduction of both the fabric and trimmings, including the bullion fringe.

✾ Trimming made by Scalamandré was used (and is still made) for the original Big Bird's legs since Jim Henson was a client.

✾ The only queen in the United States, Queen Kamehameha of Hawaii, had a fascination for tassels, which adorned her throne.

One of the most popular uses for tassels throughout history was as "key tassels" which, according to Goodman, "are always fun" - colorful, creative, and usually smaller than their more "serious" cousins. Key tassels have a very small loop at the top for attaching a key. The key, usually one of those antique skeleton-types, is inserted into its lock and the tassel hangs as a decorative accent. (You can make your own key tassel from instructions on page 84. I have attempted to imitate as closely as possible the techniques used by the factory workers at the Scalamandré factory.)

Goodman's designs in fringe and other trimmings can be found at the Metropolitan Opera House, the New York State Theatre, and various other national theaters. One of the most popular uses for fringe is as "base fringe," which is stitched along the lower edge of an easy chair to keep one's feet from damaging the upholstery. Another popular use for especially heavy bullion fringe is in home theaters, a relatively new trend for wealthy clients.

Goodman designs two complete seasons each year: Spring and Fall. The showroom samples, as well as all the custom work, are executed in Scalamandré's Long Island City factory. Most designs are created from 100% silk, from raw to cultivated, depending on the desired look. The custom trimmings range in price from $200 to $2,500 per yard. Scalamandré tassels start at $65 per tassel.

The Luxe Makers: The Scalamandré Factory

After my visit to the New York City showroom, I visited the factory in Long Island City in Queens. What the showroom provided in visual inspiration the factory provided in the amazing transformation from the conceptual design to the actual tassel, mostly custom made for each client.

Julie Kaminska was my tour guide and we started in the computer design room. Besides making wonderful tassels and trimmings, one of the company's areas of expertise is in duplicating historic textiles, as mentioned previously. Numerous labor-intensive steps are required to re-create the exact colors, textures, weight, fiber, and construction of original historic textiles, often from just a small swatch of fabric. In historic buildings, luxurious fabrics were often used as wall coverings with matching or coordinating draperies. These fabrics often run in the $250-per-yard range and the yardage required can be quite extensive. Matching the trimmings, including the tassels, is made easier these days with the advent of computer color-matching. (It was actually quite a juxtaposition to look at such old textiles duplicated with the use of such contemporary equipment.)

The Long Island City factory uses primarily 100% silk threads for their trimmings and tassels unless otherwise requested by the client. Silk not only has the best "hand" (feel and drape) for trimmings and tassels, but it also has the highest color retention capacity. As a result, when the factory dyes yellow, the richness of the fiber, combined with the depth of the color, makes for a particularly dramatic yellow.

Silk thread has the highest color retention capacity.

Although today's consumers look for the easiest and quickest way to do or make something, the philosophy at Scalamandré is to maintain an exceptional level of quality regardless of how long it may take to make the trim or tassel. This insures that the client receives exactly what he or she has ordered and expects. While we may see commercially manufactured tassel fringe in fabric stores, the fact that the tassel fringe made by Scalamandré is created from 100% silk and each tassel is created one-at-a-time by hand makes the company stand apart from the traditionally manufactured version.

To create bullion fringe, which is also used as tassel skirts, multiple spools of silk thread are combined into a *roving,* which is then tightly twisted and spooled. The

Fringe is created by hand to exact specifications.

twisted roving feeds into a bullion-making machine, which looks something like a narrow weaving loom. It consists of a loom that weaves the top (also called the selvage, the section that is enclosed in the seam of the fabric) of the bullion fringe as well as provides a decorative edge. A type of mechanical crochet hook then hooks onto the roving and pulls it back a pre-determined distance. The twisted roving is then released to double back on itself to create the bullion. Quite impressive.

A bullion-making machine.

The woven trimmings made in the factory are created using multiple pattern cards that are fed into a punch card machine that "reads" the pattern and controls the heddle selection to achieve the desired pattern. The company also has highly sophisticated, computerized looms as well, making the operation capable of both creating contemporary fabrics and trims as well as duplicating historic textiles using the same or similar equipment the originals were made with.

Lastly, I visited "Cord Alley" - a very long space where cords of all types and colors are displayed on the walls with patterning information and tassels.

Cord Alley also houses the notorious cording wheel. My first impression of this machine was that it looks like a medieval torture device, but I soon learned that it is used to create the amazing diversity of cords used in trims and tassels. The cording produced by the machine ranges from very simple double

Cords of all types and colors are displayed in Cord Alley.

ble cord to multiple cords. Its "cord master" makes the determination as to what threads and colors are used for each order and how far to position the machine down the "alley" for the desired yardage.

The historical importance of this company and its impact on the national preservation and reproduction of historic textiles is evident. It was very obvious that this family is committed to maintaining the direction, quality, and integrity of its founder.

The cording wheel.

The cord master at work.

Chapter III

Tools & Techniques of the Trade

Unique Inventions for Tassel & Fringe-Making

The best way to start this section of tools and materials, technique instruction, and patterns is to first have a definition of the tassel and fringe-making terms used in this book.

Bullion. This term is applied to one or more groups of yarn or thread that have been formed into a twisted decorative cord or fringe. The end result takes on the appearance of a barber pole-type spiral twist.

Bullion cord. This term refers to the twisted cord that is created for the dual purpose of providing a decorative way for hanging a tassel as well as the traditional method used to hold all the components of the tassel together. It is also used to refer to the spiral twisted decorative edging often found around pillows, upholstered furniture, and drapery.

Bullion fringe. The fringe made from the twisting process to create fringe is more challenging to make than standard cut-edge fringe, but the end result is particularly impressive looking. The two tools especially useful for creating bullion fringe are discussed later in the chapter.

Bullion tassel skirt. This is the skirt of a tassel that has been formed from bullion fringe. It can be made entirely from bullion fringe or can be a combination of cut and bullion or various combinations of thicknesses and colors.

Cut-skirt fringe. This description differentiates between a bullion fringe or skirt and one where the lower edges of the fringe or skirt have been cut across.

Finial. This term refers to the hard form, also called a "mold," often used as the cap or top of a tassel. Finials are often made of wood but can be made from any small container-type form. Finial-topped tassels are created very differently from soft tassels (those without a top) and are the most decorative of the two. I also refer to finials as "tassel tops" in this book.

Flounce disk. This can be a wood wheel, metal washer, bead, or other flat object that has approximately the same diameter as that of the lower edge of the finial. With the hanging cord, the flounce disk is pulled up against the lower base of the tassel, causing the tassel skirt to "flounce" by splaying out the skirt around the perimeter of the lower edge of the tassel top. This creates a more desirable look than one with the skirt hanging straight down. It also eliminates the need for the large amount of yarn or fringe that would be needed to create a similar look. Note that all tassels designs do not require a flounce disk.

Ruff. The dual-purpose "mini-skirt" that is wrapped around the lower edge of a finial either to cover the edge of a skirt that has been wrapped around the lower edge of the finial or purely as decoration. Not all tassels have ruffs, but they are usually found in the most elaborate and decorative tassels.

Tassel head. This is usually used in reference to the top part of a soft tassel and is the section through which the hanging cord is inserted.

Tassel neck. Also usually used in reference to a soft tassel. The neck of the tassel is the section that is wrapped with yarn or other material and which separates the head of the tassel from the skirt. It also serves to hold the hanging cord in place.

Tassel skirt. *See cut-skirt fringe.*

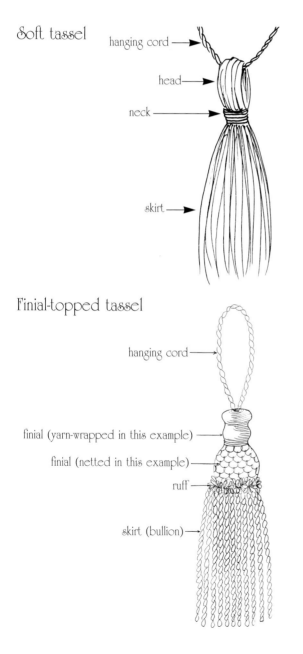

Soft tassel
- hanging cord
- head
- neck
- skirt

Finial-topped tassel
- hanging cord
- finial (yarn-wrapped in this example)
- finial (netted in this example)
- ruff
- skirt (bullion)

Tools

Note: Sources for all the tools in this chapter are listed in the Resources section on page 128.

There are many ways to create tassels, fringe, finials, and trim. I focus on the best ones - some you may never have thought could be used for that purpose. Always looking for the fastest method that produces particularly good results (what good is fast if the results are undesirable?), I poked around hardware stores, lumberyards, toy stores, flea markets, housewares stores, and, obviously, yarn and craft stores. I found tools and materials in all of those places, tested each one, and included the ones that worked best.

Detailed operating instructions for tools designed for tassel and fringe-making come with those tools, so I explain the use of those tools only briefly. However, for those tools that are not ordinarily used to make tassels, I give a more detailed explanation as to their use and, with some tools, include a photograph of the tool in use.

My favorite tools, the ones that provided the greatest assistance in making the tassels featured in this book, are: a crochet fork, the Trim Tool, the Tassel Master, an accordion (expanding) hat rack (the kind with pegs), a swift (also called a skein holder), the E-Z Twister, the Spinster or Kreinik Custom Corder, small cardboard tubes, a hand-held cordless drill, small vice, and bamboo chopsticks.

Soft Tassel, Fringe & Tassel Skirt Making Tools

Since the primary component for making tassels and fringe is yarn, thread, or cording, a description of tools used to change yarn into fringe, tassel skirts, or cording must come first. Often the type of yarn, thread, or cording you choose will determine the type of tool to use.

Since tassels have been made for at least 1,000 years, there have obviously been numerous tools used in the process, certainly varying by the culture and available resources. In this chapter, I focus on tools that are either new or newly used for this craft or those tools you can easily make yourself.

Making Soft Tassels

Soft tassels are the easiest to make.

The simplest type of tassel to make is a "soft" tassel. This tassel is made entirely of yarn as opposed to the finial-top tassel. A soft tassel is made by wrapping thread or yarn around a tool, frame, piece of cardboard, or other device until the desired thickness has been achieved. Then by tying the very top of the tassel through all thicknesses of yarn, cutting the yarn along the lower edge of the tassel, and wrapping the same or contrasting yarn around the upper quarter of the tassel, creating a "neck" and "head" of the tassel. Soft tassels are the most widely recognized type, the small ones that are most commonly available ready-made.

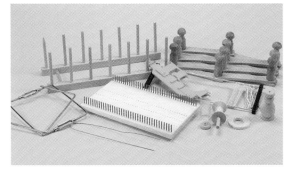

Some of the preferred tools for making tassels.

The **Trim Tool** is an ingenious tool that has most often been recommended for cutting latch-hook rug yarn, but I find it is one of the best tools for creating tassels. This plastic tool is comprised of two interlocking sections around which you wrap the yarn for the tassel. It has an opening for tying the neck of the tassel and a channel on top for tying the top, after which you unlock the two parts to release the tassel.

The Trim Tool can make 3″ to 6″ long tassels. It is very inexpensive and can be found in most yarn and craft stores. Complete instructions for making soft tassels come with the tool, but as a brief description, the tool is adjusted for the desired length for the tassel, yarn is wrapped around the frame, tied at the top and around the neck and the yarn cut at the bottom. The tool is then separated to release the tassel.

The **Tatool** is a metal frame around which you wind lengths of yarn over each other until you achieve the desired thickness. After you tie the tassel at the neck and top, you remove it by turning the screw mechanism at both sides to reduce the height of the frame and release the tassel. The basic Tatool can make 3-1/2″ to 5″ long fringe or tassel skirts. The Tatool with an extension enables you to make fringe or tassels up to 7″ long. Complete instructions for making tassels and fringe come with the Tatool.

Yes, a **folding accordion hat rack**, the kind that has a series of pegs where the uppermost part of the peg is thicker than the part that attaches to the folding strips, is an excellent tassel-making tool. A rack that is a bit "stiff" to fold is best. Pull the rack open to the desired width between the pegs, but not to its fullest width. By wrapping the yarn or cord around the pegs, you can create from three to ten of the same size tassels at the same time. I used a hat rack to create the small tassels that are around the Mosaic tassel on page 74. Complete instructions for using the folding accordion hat rack are detailed in the projects that call for using it.

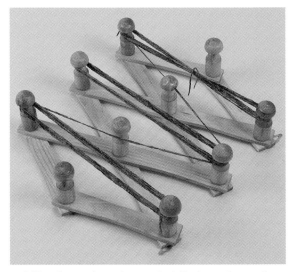

A folding hat rack works wonderfully for making soft tassels.

The **crochet fork** is similar to the Tatool but the two horizontal bars are inserted through a series of holes in the plastic side bars. With the crochet fork, you can make tassels from 1″ to 4″ long. Wrap the fork with yarn, stitch along the top edge, and remove one or both of the side bars to release the tassel. Complete instructions for making tassels using the crochet fork are included with the projects that call for using it.

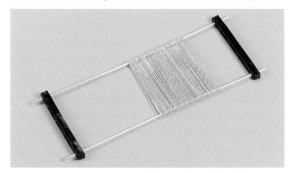

With a crochet fork, you can make tassels 1″ to 4″ long.

A **plate drying or display rack**, the kind you see in housewares stores, is another unlikely tassel-making tool. These racks are made of wood with dowels inserted vertically that are used to hold plates. The series of dowels are ideal for making identical tassels as long as you only need one length of tassel. Wrap the yarn or thread around the dowels similar to the accordion rack, tie in the center or at the ends, and remove the yarn from the dowels. Cut the ends and wrap the neck of the tassels with thread or yarn. Using a plate rack is an option when making a number of tassels such as those on the Mosaic tassel on page 74.

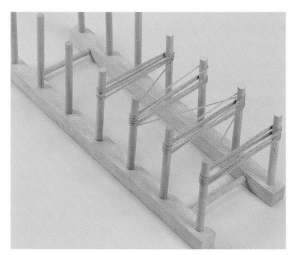

The dowels in a plate drying rack can be wrapped with tassel yarn or thread.

Making Cut-Edge Fringe & Tassel Skirts

The tools listed on page 18 are best for creating tassels and fringe with a "cut edge" as opposed to the twisted, bullion type. The fringe is intended for use on nearly any project that would be enhanced with the application of fringe. Since the tassel skirts created on these tools begin as a length of fringe (making it necessary to hide the less desirable upper edge of the fringe), they would be used with a finial top rather than with a soft tassel.

Autumn Elegance and China are two examples of cut-edge tassels. Autumn Elegance shows a finial top with cut-skirt fringe that is inserted into the opening at the bottom of the tassel. China uses a large bead cap as its finial, which has decorative jade and gold beads to "extend" the finial.

The Casbah footstool shows an example of how to combine cut-edge fringe (the cranberry color fringe) and bullion fringe (the gold color fringe) in one project.

The cut-edge tassel skirt is created as a length of fringe, which is then wound into a roll and secured with tape, wire, thread, or glue. As of this writing, there are only two tools that can accomplish this easily, the Tassel Master and a crochet fork. The rolled skirt is then inserted into the opening at the bottom of the finial. Alternatively, the fringe can be wrapped around the lower edge of a finial that has a "lip." Or you can create a tassel with both an inserted skirt as well as one wrapped around the lower edge, depending on whether or not the finial you use has a lip.

This bullion tassel skirt is inserted into the finial.

This bullion tassel skirt has a length of bullion fringe inserted into the lower edge and another section wrapped around the lower lip of the finial. The top edge of the fringe around the edge is embellished with the addition of small ribbon roses.

The **Tassel Master** is comprised of a board with a series of holes to hold specially designed pegs. The upper row of pegs always remains in Position #1. The lower four rows of pegs allow you to make tassels from 2″ to 5″ long and allow for various configurations of tassel skirts. By using the Tassel Master extension board, you can make skirts from 6″ to 10″ long. The prod-

uct works very much the same for both cut-edge and bullion. Complete instructions for making both cut-edge and bullion tassels and fringe come with Tassel Master.

The Tassel Master.

The advantage of using the Tassel Master is the ability to keep the yarn strands spaced equally. The only disadvantage is that you can only hold two strands of yarn together at once, but you can compensate for this by making two lengths of fringe and doubling them.

You can easily make cut-edge with a **crochet fork** too. You can use the 11″ width (excluding the side bars) by wrapping the yarn around the bars to the desired density and, using a zipper foot (zigzag stitch is ideal but not essential), sew just under the top bar. Then just remove the plastic side bars, slide off the fringe, and cut the bottom edges. Complete instructions and illustrations for using a crochet fork to make tassels are detailed in the projects that call for using one.

The only disadvantage I found with the crochet fork for making cut-edge fringe is the difficulty in maintaining even spacing between the yarns. However, if that is not critical to your design, the crochet fork will work quite well.

Sliding the yarn off a crochet fork.

Twisting Tools & Methods

Twisting tools for twisting yarn and thread to create bullion fringe and tassel skirts.

To make bullion fringe, bullion tassel skirts, or bullion hanging cords, the yarns, threads, or cords must be twisted. Twisting a quantity of yarn or threads for making fringe or tassel skirts requires slightly different tools than those for making a hanging cord, since hanging cords require much shorter lengths of yarn. The twisting tools for making fringe and hanging cords are described separately below.

The following three tools are for twisting almost unlimited amounts of yarn or thread.

The **E-Z Twister** is my hands-down favorite twisting tool. It can be found in fabric stores and catalogs and is the reason I asked Alma Gulsby, its inventor, to be a part of this book (see page 124). You will need a sewing machine with a bobbin winder on the top of the machine. Attach the special E-Z bobbin and spool to the bobbin winder, tie the yarn or thread to the hole in the spool, and bring it up through the notch in the top of the spool. By holding the yarn

The E-Z Twister.

or thread taut and pressing the foot pedal, you quickly twist it. Then remove the yarn from the notch and by pressing the foot pedal again, you wind the twisted yarn onto the spool. Repeat the twisting and winding process to fill the spool. The E-Z Twister comes with complete instructions for twisting the yarn or thread for creating bullion fringe. It also comes with patterns.

The **Spinning Spool** is a component of the Tassel Master. Yarns are twisted by securing them to the spool, spinning the spool until you achieve the desired tension, then winding the twisted yarn or thread onto the spool and securing it with the special spool clip that comes with the Tassel Master. Continue the spinning and winding process until you have the desired amount of yarn. The Tassel Master includes complete instructions for using the Spinning Spool.

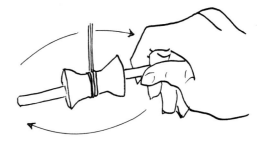

The Spinning Spool is a component of Tassel Master.

You can make your own **extra large spinning spool** for twisting cording, thick yarn, or groups of yarns. Purchase two 1-3/4″ wooden wheels and a dowel the diameter of the hole in the wheels. You will also need four small rubber bands. Mark the dowel at 10″, 7″, and 3″. Cut the dowel at the 10″ mark. Slide one rubber band down to 1/2″ beyond the 7″ mark. Slide on one of the wheels and the second rubber band. Then slide the third rubber band to the 3″ mark, slide on the second wheel and the last rubber band. (Alternatively, you could use tape instead of glue or you could glue the wheels to the dowel at the 7″ and 3″ marks.) You could also use bobbins used for spinning wheels, but they are a bit expensive and may need additional weighting to be sure they are in balance. Use this large spool in the same way you would use the Spinning Spool. For those readers who do not have a Tassel Master, tape the yarn or threads to the dowel in the center of the spool and spin the spool using one of the end dowels as the "spinner."

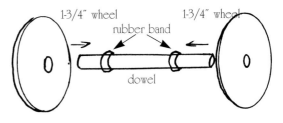

The following tools are used to twist a fixed or shorter length of yarn or thread and are primarily used to make hanging cords, for embellishing a tassel finial, or for making an overskirt.

To use these tools and methods, you will need to have a hook affixed to a wall or grid (or you can use any number of substitutes) on which you will hook the yarn, which is held in tension while being corded. (Don't hook the yarn on your best vase and expect it to stay upright and intact.) Many instructions recommend using a doorknob, but it is difficult to remove tightly twisted cording from a standard doorknob. *Note:* You can also use the E-Z Twister, the Spinning Spool, or the Tassel Master, but use shorter lengths of yarn.

The **Spinster** and **Kreinik Custom Corder** are inexpensive (under $10) twisting tools that look like a toy hand drill with a cup hook inserted in the end. These handy tools make creating hanging cord and other bullion accents very fast.

Spinster or
Custom
Corder

The makers of the Custom Corder recommend using a 2-oz. weight which is slipped on the twisted yarn before the ends are joined to create bullion cord. The result is more evenly distributed twists in the bullion cord. The Spinster and Custom Corder come with detailed instructions on their use. The **Leonardo Rope Maker** is a wood-based twisting tool with five hooks that will twist from one to five groups of yarns at one time for making multi-color bullion cord. This tool comes with complete instructions for its use.

weight attached
to twisted yarn

After using one of these tools to twist the yarn, tie the ends in a knot and hook the unknotted loop to a wall hook. You might insert a pencil, chopstick, or short knitting needle into the knotted end, and holding the yarn taut, rotate the pencil to create a tightly twisted bullion. You can also use a manually operated **egg beater** to achieve similar results.

Lastly, you can also use a **hand-held drill** with a cup hook inserted into the end, but take care not to twist the yarn too tightly since an electric drill can speed up this process almost too much. You can also use a non-electric drill, which may be the better choice. These are great flea-market finds.

Making Bullion

The fringe around this covered box is an example of bullion fringe.

Bullion is so interesting to use in decorating and so much fun to make, especially if you have some time-saving tools. Bullion is made from one or a few yarns, threads, or cords held together and twisted to the desired tension, which are then released one by one and allowed to double back on themselves to create the desired bullion effect.

Just as for cut-skirt fringe, bullion fringe is made in sections the width of the board or frame, then sewn or otherwise joined together to the desired length, or it can be made in one continuous length. You can use either the Tassel Master or a crochet fork to make bullion fringe. The instructions that come with the Tassel Master will tell you how to wrap the bullion to create fringe. To use the crochet fork you must first twist the yarn, wrap it around the frame, then sew through the very top of the fringe using a zipper foot. The upper and lower rods are removed and the bullion is automatically created.

The Tassel Master method of making bullion is a simple two-step process. First, using the Spinning Spool, twist the yarns by spinning the spool then winding the twisted yarn onto the spool, securing them with the special clip that comes with the Tassel Master. (You can also use the E-Z Twister to twist the yarns or threads.) You can make skirts from 6″ to 10″ long by using the Tassel Master extension board.

Wrap the twisted yarns around the Tassel Master pegs.

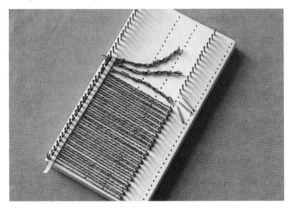

Apply tape as shown. Then either remove the pegs one at a time or lift the lower edge of the yarn around the peg off the peg, allowing it to twist back on itself to create the bullion. Remove the bullion from the board.

A 10″ long bullion cord knotted into a circle and threaded with a flounce disk using the threading wire (that comes with the kit). Bullion fringe is wrapped around the threading wire which is inserted into the lower edge of the finial and through the top. Cording pulls the flounce disk up, pulling the skirt as it goes.

If you use the **crochet fork**, you will need to twist the yarns or threads before wrapping them around the entire length of the fork. Stitch through the top of the twisted yarn or thread, just under the upper bar, then remove the plastic side bars and slide off the bullion fringe, one by one.

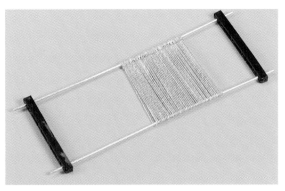

Twist the threads before wrapping them around the crochet fork.

Remove the plastic side bar and slide the threads off.

Making Finials

Ready-made wood finials come with a hole drilled from top to bottom.

I recommend starting your first experience in making finial-topped tassels by choosing a ready-made wood finial with a hole drilled from top to bottom.

Wood candle cups, available at most craft stores, are also suitable since most have a hole already drilled through. If you want to use other types of wood finials, especially large ones, you will usually need to drill a hole through the finial, which is a very simple process. Other, more unusual types of finials are described and pictured in Chapter VIII, "Terrific Finial Tassels."

Since wood is one of the most ideal materials for making finials, here are some of the wood parts that can be used.

Some of the especially easy finial-topped tassels in this book call for one or more of the protective plastic or rubber caps used on the bottom of chairs. An awl, a hammer, and a dowel the size of the cap are the only tools you need. Insert the dowel in the cap and punch a hole in the center bottom (top of finial) using the awl and hammer.

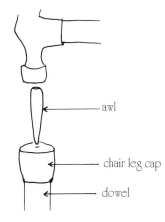

awl

chair leg cap

dowel

If using undrilled wood parts or other caps or containers, you will need a **hand-held drill** (corded or cordless) for making the hole for the hanging cord, and a small **vice** (very inexpensive) to hold the wood piece or cap upright while drilling (and to save your hands from slips of the drill). Be sure to protect the wood piece by attaching **felt** to the sides of the inside of the vice or wrapping the piece with felt or other protective fabric. If you plan to drill a number of finials, you may want to consider purchasing an

inexpensive (under $20) drill press converter tool for converting your drill temporarily into a drill press. Most woodworking stores carry this tool, which is also invaluable for making sure the hole you are drilling is straight. The drill you use should have a 1/4″ bit, the most common size used to drill through finials. You can also purchase **borer drill bits**, which bore a wide hole in the bottom of a wood piece so you can insert the tassel skirt in the bottom of the finial.

You may want to consider purchasing or designating a simple table to use just for drilling since it is advisable to affix the vice to a table or board clamped to a table. Suzann Thompson uses a Workmate table that has a number of features. I use an old collapsible table. Be sure the table you use has a "real" top (not sturdy cardboard or flimsy chipboard). The top of an old door, the kind with a strip of rubber (which helps to hold the door in place while you're pulling on the tool) along the top, makes an ideal table when set on two sturdy sawhorses.

Decorating Finials

If you have the right tools, decorating finials can be an easy and fun part of the process.

The best way to hold the finial for decorating is with an old set of hand knitting needles, chopsticks, or a 1/4″ or smaller diameter dowel that has been slightly sharpened in a pencil sharpener but is still blunt. The advantage of using old knitting needles is that the paint and glue are more easily removed from the metal or plastic than from the bamboo or wood. Having various sizes of "holders" enables you to have a ready holder for whatever size finial you are decorating.

You will also need a weighted base with varying sized holes drilled in the top. A block of discarded wood with various holes the diameter of your "holders" drilled in it is great. Or you could use a terra cotta flowerpot with a weighted base (rocks work fine) and filled with packing foam in which you can insert the chopsticks or knitting needles (the double-pointed ones work best here). You can also stick the holders in a weighted cup. These holders are invaluable when you need to set the spray adhesive or let the paint on the finial dry.

A weighted flowerpot works well to hold finials while decorating.

logs and specialty electrical supply stores. Its clip "hands" can be swiveled in any direction, as can the elbow where the two clips are joined. It's ideal for holding cording, yarn, wire, etc., while you attach mini-tassels or any type of embellishment. The clips will hold nearly any thickness of cording, no matter how thin.

The handy "third arm" tool will hold any thickness of cording.

The double-clip holder is also excellent for holding the tops of soft tassels while you work on embellishing the neck or adding other decorations.

If you can't locate a double-clip holder, you can make your own holding tool. Although it won't be quite as versatile as the double-clip one, it will certainly be of value.

Tools for Holding Cording & Soft Tassels

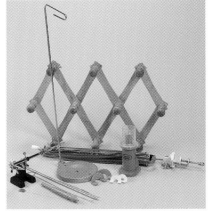

Some of the more contemporary tools for making various tassel components.

These tools are very helpful when you don't have a human assistant willing to spend time holding cording while you add tassels or pompons. (Do any of us really have such a person?)

One of the most ingenious tools I have found is the double-clip holder, also known as the "third arm." It can be found in jewelry cata-

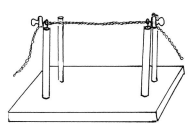

Make your own holding tool. Using four dowels instead of two allows you to use it as a jig for making mini-tassels or pompoms too.

Close-up of the top of the dowel.

You will need a wood base approximately 5″ x 10″ x 1/2″ (although the measurements do not need to be precise), two 3/8″ to 1/2″ diameter dowels 6″ long (four if making the jig version shown), two screw-eyes with openings to accommodate the maximum size cording you plan to use, two spring or binder clips, a pair of pliers, and a drill with a bit the size of the dowels and one a bit smaller than the screw-eyes screw.

Drill two holes 6″ to 8″ apart in the center of

the base. Using a vice to hold the dowels upright, drill a hole in the top center of each of the dowels. Affix the dowels in the holes of the base. With the pliers, screw the screw-eyes into the tops of the dowels. Thread the cording into the screw-eyes and secure with a clip at each end.

If you make the base a bit larger and add two more dowels, forming a "square" of dowels, the device can also be used as a jig for making mini-tassels or pompons. To make mini-tassels or fringe, wind the yarn around the outside perimeter of all four dowels. Then follow the instructions for using the umbrella swift (see Southwestern Tassel instructions on page 68), but slide the yarn off the tops of the dowels when you have completed the yarn winding.

If you simply need a device to hold your tassel while you "primp" it, comb the skirt, or otherwise work on a finished (or nearly finished) tassel, a **serger thread cone holder** is ideal. The base is weighted and the hook that stands upright for holding thread for feeding into a serger is the ideal height for holding a tassel of nearly any weight (sometimes finials can be heavy). You can buy serger thread cone holders at fabric or sewing machine stores or through sewing supply catalogs. **Ornament holders** also work for this purpose, but they are not very tall and need a weight at the base for stability.

Making Knitted Cording

A tassel skirt made from three strands of embroidery floss knitted on the Magicord Machine.

Knitted cording makes some of the easiest and most attractive fringe and tassel skirts, especially when making larger tassels. There are four ways and tools you can use to make knitted cording (also called idiot-cord or I-cord by knitters). I've listed these from the fastest to the most time-consuming.

The **Magicord Machine** is actually a small, circular knitting machine that creates knitted cording from thin yarns and threads using the four latch-hooked needles on its top to knit each stitch by turning the handle on the side of the machine. If you plan to make many yards of cording, this is the best way to knit it. The Magicord Machine comes with detailed instructions on making knitted cording, including making a tassel skirt.

If you have a **knitting machine** you can make knitted cording by following the instructions that come with your machine. Since each machine is different, it is not feasible to list all techniques for all machines here.

If you are a hand knitter you can knit I-cord using two double pointed **hand knitting needles**. Cast on four stitches. Knit across. Slide the stitches to the opposite end of the needles and knit the same four stitches. Yes, the yarn will be pulled across the four knitted stitches, but when the cording has been knitted, the cording will even out.

You can also use a **spool knitter** or **Knitty Knobby,** which is a spool with four nails in the top. Many of us used these as kids to make dollhouse rugs and hair ties. Most of us remember how we learned to knit on the spool knitter by wrapping the yarn around the four nails and looping the new yarn through the yarn around the nails to form knitted stitches. Spool knitters today are made in plastic and wood and come with complete instructions (but I know you all remember how to do this).

Threading Tools

There are many ways to insert a hanging cord and each method is described in the instructions for the individual projects in the book.

The most common way to insert a hanging cord is by using a **threading wire**. A threading wire is usually just a standard 22 or 20 gauge stem wire found at most craft stores. After you fold it in half, you will use it to hold the hanging cord (and usually the flounce disk, which can be anything from a wooden wheel to a metal washer) and thread it through the bottom of the tassel. This serves to flounce out the tassel skirt as well as serves as a holder for the tassel.

Another tool that is very effective for drawing through cords or catching errant threads is a **loop turner**. This device consists of a 10˝ long wire with a ring on one end and a latch hook on the other. It functions by inserting the turner through a narrow opening, grasping the cord or thread with the hook, and drawing it back through the opening, thereby closing the latch so the hook doesn't catch on anything else while it's being drawn through the hole. It's also exceptionally good for pulling bullion cording through the heads of soft tassels.

Using a loop turner to pull cord through the head of a soft tassel.

A **yarn darner** and **weaving needle** are excellent for threading thinner cords through the center of a finial. The yarn darner is just an "over-sized" tapestry needle and is made in plastic and steel. The eye is particularly large to accommodate thin cords or hand knitting yarns. A weaving needle is about double the length of the more common yarn darner and similar in diameter.

Making Mini-Tassels or Pompoms

Mini-tassels make for a special accent in this tassel.

Pompons can comprise a tassel accent or the entire skirt.

Among the most popular embellishments for tassels and overskirts are mini-tassels or pompons. While very visually appealing, they can take time to make. However, the following tools make the process much easier and faster.

A **spool holder** is invaluable for holding spooled threads to keep them from tangling while you wind or otherwise use them. There are a number of spool holders available, but one that has four or five pegs of varying thicknesses (to accommodate different types of spooled threads) is particularly good so you can use various yarns when making your tassel. Similar to the cording holder described earlier, you can wind yarn around the perimeter of the spool holder to create mini-tassels or pompons.

A typical spool holder.

The **umbrella swift** or **skein holder** is a device familiar to knitters and weavers who purchase yarn in traditional skeins or hanks. Normally, the swift is opened to a size large enough to hold a skein of yarn for winding into a ball. For tassel-making purposes, the skein holder is used to wind yarn or thread onto it for making a number of mini-tassels. This is accomplished by using the handle on top of the swift and rotating it to wind on the yarn or threads, or you can manually spin the swift. Cut a piece of cardboard or measure off on a ruler twice the desired

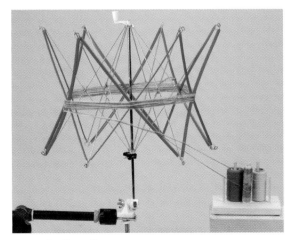

An umbrella swift.

length of the tassel or pompon thickness. After you have wound the amount of yarn for your tassels or pompons, tie the yarn together in equal lengths and remove from the swift by reducing the circumference in the same way you'd take down an umbrella. Then just cut the yarn bunches evenly between the ties. This is how I made the Southwestern Tassel on page 68.

More detailed directions for making mini-tassels and fringe can be found in those projects that utilize them in their design.

You can make a jig as described on page 23 and tie the yarns as you would if using the swift. You can also use the plate drying rack to make tassels and pompons. The accordion peg rack can also be used in the same way as the jig or umbrella swift.

If you are planning to make just a few pompons, the **Pompom Maker** from Clover is the best tool. The smallest pompon that can be made using this tool is 1-1/4″ diameter.

Making Ruffs

A typical ruff used around the lower edge of a wood finial.

Ruffs, the decorative, usually fluffy embellishment around the lower edge of the finial, both visually and often actually join the tassel finial to its skirt. Traditionally, ruffs were one of the most time-consuming parts of the tassel to make, but with the use of today's tools, they are particularly easy to make.

Each project that has a ruff around the tassel will describe the making technique, but here are some of the tools you will need.

A **crochet fork** works well for creating a ruff, since the rods can be closely positioned, enabling you to sew through the threads or yarns wrapped around the rods.

An easy and effective way to create a ruff is by using **two dowels** of the same or different di-

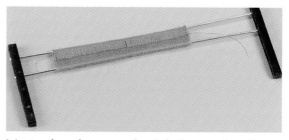

Moving the rods on a crochet fork close together allows you to make a ruff.

ameters. The 1/8″ to 3/8″ diameter dowels should be between 10″ and 12″ long. The ruff around the Brasilia tassel on page 86 was created this way but using an even larger dowel for a more dramatic look.

You can also crochet a ruff using a loop stitch. Small (steel sizes up to size C) **crochet hooks** are best when using thin yarns, which are most commonly used for tassels.

Another interesting way to create ruffs is by pushing or hooking thread or narrow ribbon through 7-mesh **plastic canvas**. I used this method to make the Key Tassel on page 84, but made the whole skirt, not just the ruff, this way.

In my opinion, the best way to create a ruff is by using a **punch needle**. These have been popular over the years for creating pictures or tapestries using a tufting technique, which is also called punch needle embroidery. To create a ruff, set the needle length to medium to long, make three to four rows of punch the length of the circumference of the tassel finial, and, voilà, you have one of the best and most quickly made ruffs. The ruffs around the Bridal Tassel (page 88) and the Southwestern Tassel (page 68) were made using a punch needle.

punch needle

Adhesives

While this category is really not classified as tools, a review of adhesives is definitely in order. Tapes and glues serve a critical function in tassel making.

The most important glue for adhering fringe, for securing knots, or for catching in errant strands of yarn is **clear-drying fabric glue**. My favorite is Fabri-Tac since it dries quickly, especially nice for folks like me who have too little patience to wait any more than a few minutes for glue to dry.

Adhesives helpful in embellishing and securing tassel components.

The most important type of tape for making fringe is **removable masking tape**, such as drafting tape. It is sufficiently adhesive to hold bullion fringe and leaves no residue when it is removed, which must be done after sewing through the top of the fringe if you plan to wash the project.

The most important adhesive for making tassel skirts is 1/4″ wide **double-faced tape**, such as the type that comes in the Tassel Master kit. This tape can be purchased separately under the brand name Peel 'n Stick. The very high adhesion of this tape virtually guarantees your tassel will not come apart. Be careful that the tape doesn't adhere to anything unintended. *Note:* This tape is not washable (but who washes finial-topped tassels anyway?).

The most important adhesive for applying anything other than paint, stain, or découpage to a finial is **spray adhesive**. Stick a finial on the pointed end of a chopstick or old knitting needle, put on a pair of gloves, and spray the finial. It's best to spray into a large box with one of the flaps closed to keep the spray from the floor, walls, kids, etc. (If you don't use the box idea, you'll understand why I mention the kids.) When using spray adhesive, try to wear rubber gloves on both hands since the spray is not easily removed from hands. You will need to apply a relatively heavy coat but without getting a gooey build-up. Let the glue set at least an hour, since whatever you will be applying to the finial will adhere much better if you wait. Use the hour to make your tassel skirt.

If you are making fringe using the masking tape and sewing method, and if you are not a sewer, you could try **Steam-a-Seam 2**. Press one side to the fringe (instead of sewing across the top), remove the paper covering the second side and press the fringe, tape side down, to the

wrong side of the fabric. *Note:* You should not use this technique with thick corded fringe until you have tested the adhering quality of the tape with the cording you are using.

Although **wire** cannot technically be called an adhesive, when making tassels it functions in a very similar way - to hold or secure tassel skirts, ruffs, or even embellishments to the tassel finial. The best wire to use is thin but strong (28 to 20 gauge) wire that is available on spools at most craft or hardware stores.

Grooming Tools

To be sure your tassel looks its best, it's important to have a few handy finishing tools on hand. Since so many fibers have previously been wound, skeined, coned, or otherwise packaged, they can contain kinks, folds, or frays. Keep a good **steamer** or **steam iron** handy.

While you steam your tassel, comb it to straighten the threads or yarns. I find the best tool for accomplishing this is a **hair pick**, the plastic kind with the thick, wide teeth. The teeth are sufficiently spaced not to catch most bullion and close enough to make fine threads straight. To comb out very thin threads and 6-strand embroidery floss, especially when you want to comb out multiple colors, a **hair comb** with fine teeth is best. Actually, one with a long, thin handle, which can be used to separate and straighten thick bullion cording, is best.

Lastly, if you are blending two or more colors of cotton embroidery floss together, a fine but firm hairbrush is very helpful.

There are many more tassel and fringe-making tools for you to discover. I'd love to hear about your "finds" and, who knows, perhaps you'll invent the next tassel-making tool.

A variety of combs help straighten tassel threads.

Chapter IV

Yarns & Threads

Where Color & Content Tell All

*S*ince you can use such a wide range of materials to make fringe, tassel skirts, and cords, the instructions for each project specify the actual yarns or threads used. A listing of suppliers selling many types of yarn can be found in Resources on page 128. However, often the best source for yarns is the "odd lot" bin in most yarn shops. These bins or baskets contain single balls of yarn from non-matching dye lots, discontinued yarns or colors, or the odd remaining ball returned by a knitter. Independent yarn shops carry such a wide variety of yarns that you are bound to find just the right type for tassel-making - and it's usually on sale to boot!

In the project instructions, the specific colors are listed as shown in the photograph, however these are to be used only as a point of reference and to give you an idea of how many colors are best for the design. If your color scheme is different from that used in the photograph, a good tip is to purchase a number of skeins of embroidery floss in the color ranges that interest you and play with them at home, matching or contrasting them to your decorating scheme. Although all the materials may not be available in these exact colors, it will give you a guide.

Some of the most commonly and widely available yarns and threads used for making tassel skirts and for doing yarn-wrapping on finials. These include (on the larger spools from left to right): punch embroidery yarn, rayon chenille, matte rayon, chainette, rayon crochet thread, hand-dyed rayon bouclé yarn, fancy rayon/cotton hand knitting yarn, acrylic crochet yarn, Multi's Embellishing Yarn, Ribbon Floss. Yarns shown flat: silk embroidery ribbon, rayon embroidery floss, cotton embroidery floss, metallic floss, perle cotton (2 sizes), wool Persian yarn, and wire-edged ribbon.

Traditional Tassel Yarns

The type of yarn most commonly used in small, commercially-made tassels is called "chainette," which is usually made from acetate. This yarn hangs particularly well and rarely seems to crush or wrinkle, but it is difficult to find in small quantities. However, any rayon or silk blend (or other fiber that hangs well), even some acrylics, are excellent choices.

There are a number of spinners of rayon yarns listed in Resources on page 128 that make especially good tassel and fringe-making yarns. Some of my best finds have come from the stash of yarns I've been saving over the years. I even ripped out an old sweater to re-use the yarn. These days it is easy to find rayon embroidery floss, which hangs almost as well as acetate chainette.

Chainette yarn (acetate or rayon), the most common yarn used in commercially made tassels, has excellent drape and shape retention.

Cotton Embroidery Floss

Cotton embroidery floss is tempting to use because of the wide color range available. It works for hanging cording and accents, but can be "sticky," meaning the strands of yarn tend to catch on or stick to each other and not hang as straight as yarn made from other fibers when used for the tassel skirt or fringe.

This tassel skirt is made with knitted cording of cotton embroidery floss.

One of the best ways to use cotton embroidery floss is to split the skein of floss into two 3-strand lengths and tie them together end to end (most tassels require from three to five skeins). Using your tool of choice, knit the floss into cording, then make it into bullion fringe or tassel skirts. Cotton floss used in this way does not tend to stick to itself. You can also blend cotton and rayon floss. The rayon helps the tassel drape and the cotton gives it body.

Acrylic & Wool Yarns

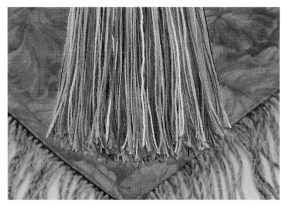

A cut-skirt tassel using acrylic punch yarn.

Most acrylic yarns are a bit too thick and sticky to use for traditional tassels, but Lustersheen is a particularly good beginner yarn to use since it is easy to hold, to twist, it "behaves," it comes in a range of colors, it is inexpensive, and it hangs well. Its only drawback is its lack of luster.

A tassel using a combination of acrylic crochet yarn as its underskirt and narrow (1/8″ and 1/4″ wide) satin ribbon as the overskirt.

Some of the most interesting tassels can be made using very fluffy yarns, especially for making pompon key tassels (see Pompon Key Tassel on page 84), fluffy bullion fringe, bouncy mini-tassels (see Southwestern Tassel on page 68), or full skirt tassels (see Autumn Elegance on page 112). Acrylic punch embroidery yarn or thin knitting machine yarn is ideal for these kinds of tassels. You can also use 100% wool crewel (also called Persian) yarn since it comes in so many colors and on small skeins. Just be sure to separate the plies and brush it out a bit before making it into tassels.

Rayon Yarns

Since rayon has properties very similar to silk, it is often confused with silk due to it luster, color intensity, and draping qualities. Rayon yarns have become increasingly popular over the years but the lustrous kinds tend to have "a mind of their own" and can be difficult to handle if not secured properly. Knots made in lustrous rayon tend to come undone, so must be secured with a drop of glue. Examples of lustrous rayon yarn and threads are crochet thread, embroidery floss, and bunka yarn.

Matte rayon yarn is exceptionally wonderful to work with and comes in a wide range of colors, although it's available only by mail from the company that makes it and only on cones. It has very good strength, drapes well, and is easy to handle.

Chenille rayon looks similar to acrylic chenille but performs very differently. The rayon yarn hangs particularly well, while the acrylic is very sticky and does not drape well, so be sure you purchase the rayon type. Acrylic chenille also cannot be cut, since it will shed and the chenille will turn into a few strands of thread. Rayon chenille can be either cut or twisted and it will not shed or lose its shape.

Rayon is often used in blended yarns, especially with cotton. Multi's Embellishment Yarn is a perfect example of this. This is a multi-color rayon/cotton blend yarn with the fullness of cotton and the drape of rayon. It can be used for cut-skirt or bullion tassels. There are other rayon/cotton blend yarns on the market as well. Check the Resources listing on page 128.

This cut-skirt tassel was made from two shades of rayon chenille yarn.

This tassel skirt was made with Multi's Embellishment Yarn corded on a Magicord Machine and made into bullion fringe. The upper and lower thirds of the finial are wrapped with bullion-corded Multi's. Beads were strung with Multi's and allowed to hang as decoration.

Sewing Threads

You can change the appearance of the yarn or thread or use thread not ordinarily used for making tassels or fringe by using rayon sewing or embroidery thread. Using the Magicord Machine, you can knit two to four strands of sewing thread into cording and then make it into bullion fringe. The results are quite spectacular since so many of these threads are available in multi-colors and metallics.

A tassel made from two strands of rayon sewing embroidery thread knitted on a Magicord Machine and made into bullion fringe.

Another way of "making" yarn for use in tassel-making is by serging threads through your serger without fabric. This technique was devised by Patti Jo Larson for the *America Sews* television show.

Using sewing threads without cording them first may create a very fly-away tassel since the threads, being so thin, are likely to be quite wispy.

Silk Yarns

Traditionally, all tassels and fringe were made from 100% silk. These days, silk is more difficult to find, primarily because of its high price tag. However, if you are making a particularly special tassel, you may want to treat yourself to silk. Silk is the fiber of choice for all historical tassels used from the ancient Chinese times through the present day. It is the "cashmere" of the decorating world. Silk has the unique properties of superb color absorption and reflection, of exceptional drape as well as fullness and of that *je ne sais quoi* when it comes to its feel - that silk "crunch" that speaks of the highest quality fiber used in home decorating.

There are a number of companies that sell undyed and dyed silk threads and yarn if you would like to make an heirloom tassel.

Out-of-the-Ordinary "Yarns"

Experiment with unusual materials when making the tassel skirt or fringe. Try working with ribbon, either standard or wire-edged, loopy doll hair or mohair yarn, dried flowers, beads, feathers, suede or leather - you can even use a doily or fancy handkerchief as a tassel skirt. I've even unraveled the edges of fabric to use in a tassel when I wanted the tassel to coordinate with the fabric and the color in the fabric was unusual and impossible to find. You can use this technique to get yarn to wrap around the neck of the tassel to perfectly match your color scheme.

A tassel made using an underskirt of fringed Polarfleece.

Handy Tassel-Making Tips

❧ If you plan to use a hand knitting yarn, be sure to check its ply, especially if you plan to make it into bullion. You will need to twist the yarn in the direction of the existing twist.

❧ Apply a dot of fabric glue to all knots and snip close to the knot.

❧ If you twist yarn and put it on a spool but don't plan to make it into fringe right away, twist the yarn with a strand of sewing thread in a matching color held with the yarn. This helps keep the yarn from losing its twist (which it can do if left twisted for more than 24 hours). I learned this the hard way when, after twisting yards of yarn, I put it down for a day or two. When I went to make it into bullion fringe, the yarn sagged out of shape.

❧ To calculate the amount of yarn or thread necessary to make 4″ long bullion fringe, use this example. From one 40-yard spool of Multi's Embellishment Yarn, you will get 30˝ of fringe, using a 3-strand thickness and the Tassel Master. ✳ If you plan to use a thick yarn or multiple threads for making bullion fringe, remember the heavier the yarn, the fewer twists you should make in the yarn before winding it to make the bullion.

Summary

Yarns with Exceptional Drape

✳ Silk threads and cording
✳ Rayon crochet thread
✳ Rayon knitting yarns
✳ Rayon chenille
✳ Matte rayon yarn
✳ Rayon embroidery floss
✳ Chainette (rayon or acetate)
✳ Rayon or blended sewing thread
✳ Acrylic crochet yarn or thread
✳ Multi's Embellishment Yarn

Fluffy Yarns

✳ Acrylic punch embroidery yarn
✳ Wool crewel yarn
✳ Many types of hand knitting yarns

Specialty Yarns

✳ Metallic yarns and threads
✳ Mercerized (shiny) cotton yarn
✳ Multi's Embellishment Yarn
✳ Loopy doll's hair
✳ Handy-dyed yarns
✳ Thin ribbon
✳ Ribbon Floss

If you plan to make a quantity of tassels or fringe, manufacturer's close-outs can be found in fairly large spools (approximately a pound or be-tween 1,000 and 2,000 yards). You could use thin, coned knitting machine yarn available in many colors and fibers. Even if you use only a fraction of a cone or large spool of yarn, the cost of the spool is usually relatively low, especially compared to the price of finished tassels or bullion fringe. The investment in the yarn is well worth its cost.

With the advent of the Internet, many manufacturers have opened websites and sell directly to the public. This also helps them sell off discontinued colors and helps to familiarize the consumer with a product that otherwise would not be known.

How to Care for Your Tassels & Fringe

If you are investing money into materials and spending time creating your tassels, you will want to know how to care for your creations. This depends on the type of materials and the type of adhesives you used. Normally, yarn tassels are washable if the yarn is washable. If you use alternative-type finials (such as those made from rubber or plastic), they may be washable if you use fabric glue or any glue that will not wash out. (Do not use any type of tacky glue if you plan to wash your project.) This is especially critical for light-colored yarns and threads.

Be sure to check (and retain) the ball band of the yarn or other packaging information on the yarn or thread you are using to be sure it is washable, especially if you are planning to use the tassel on a washable throw or pillow. Washability is primarily a factor for soft tassels since finial-topped tassels are traditionally not meant to be washed.

Traditionally, silk, rayon, and other luxury fibers are not to be washed, but this can be overcome by washing a piece of the yarn before you make it into a tassel. Acetate yarn (often used to make chainette yarn) is definitely not washable, so keep this in mind before you make tassels from chainette.

Ideally, remove finial-topped tassels before you have the project dry cleaned. When you dry clean a project that has tassels permanently attached, be sure to have the dry cleaner wrap them with protective sheeting first.

Chapter V

Hanging Cords

Pulling It All Together

The hanging cord is a primarily functional component of all tassels. The cord can range from a very simple single bullion all the way to an elaborately wrapped, beaded, or otherwise embellished variety. Since the focus of this book is making the finial and skirt parts of the tassel (which, in my opinion, are the most enjoyable parts of tassel-making), I stick to the most basic types of cords. However, in the instructions for the Sophistication Tassel on page 71, I include information for making a wrapped double bullion cord, which is significantly easier than it looks.

To make it easier to read the patterns and refer back to instructions, in each pattern I note the type of hanging cord that is used. The basic types of hanging cords are: single bullion, double bullion, triple bullion, quadruple bullion (and so on).

Left to right: Hanging cords in single to seven bullion.

The size of the tassel, the diameter of the hole through the finial, and the thickness of the yarn or cording you use will determine the type of cord as well as the number of strands of yarn or thread you can use for the hanging cord.

Making Bullion Hanging Cords

There are a number of twisting tools you can use to make bullion cording (refer to page 19 to review). To make multiple-bullion cords, I use one of the manual twisters, the Spinster or Kreinik Custom Corder. I use a plate-drying rack clamped to a table or sturdy board to hold the twisted cords, one for each length of bullion. You can also do this with pencils or chopsticks, but you will need a weight to hold down the twisted yarns.

Single Bullion Cord

The amount of yarn necessary for a particular length of cording varies, depending on the thickness of the yarn and the tightness of the twist. However, for most purposes, to get an 18″ long cord (before it is doubled for hanging), you will need to start with approximately 2-1/2 yards of yarn or group of yarns. For example, 2-yard lengths of three strands of chainette held together will produce a 14″ long cord. When joined together into a circle and knotted, the length of the loop exclusive of the knot is 5″.

1. Cut the yarn to the desired length or the length called for in the project instructions.
2. Bring the ends together and knot to form a circle.
3. Place the loop end (not the knotted end) in a hook mounted on a pegboard, wall, or grid.

4. Insert the hook of the twisting device in the knotted end of the yarn and, under tension, twist the yarns to the desired tightness. You can test this by holding a section of the twisted yarns between two fingers and relaxing the yarn, letting it double back on itself.

5. When you have achieved the desired tightness, bring the knotted end to the loop end, making sure you keep the twisted yarns under tension. (Kreinik has solved this with a weight that assures your cording will be evenly distributed once it completes its twisting. You can add your own weight with a 2-oz. fishing weight painted to cover the lead.)

6. When you have joined the ends, release the cording, letting it double back on itself.

7. Knot the ends together to keep the cording from unraveling. You may want to sew or apply glue to the knots in rayon or other slippery yarns to keep them from coming undone.

Double Bullion Cord

This cording is easy to make and very professional looking. The calculations for yarn are less for each group twisted, however, so test the technique first. You should start with nearly twice the length of cording but the thickness of a double bullion will equal that of a single bullion since it does not double back on itself.

1. Cut two equal lengths of yarn or yarn groups to be twisted separately.

2. Make the first cord following Steps 2 through 4 for single bullion, but do not join the ends.

3. You can leave the twisting device in the cord or remove it. Secure the tension of both by placing a weight on the yarn close to the twisting device, looping the end over a fixed dowel, or securing it to a table or other flat surface with a piece of strong tape.

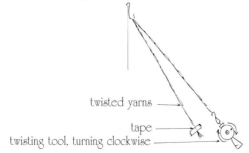

twisted yarns

tape

twisting tool, turning clockwise

4. Again, repeat Steps 2 through 4 for single bullion with the second length of yarn or group of yarns.

5. Maintaining the tension of both groups of twisted yarns, put the first twisted yarn together with the second and work a reverse twist until the cording no longer twists on itself.

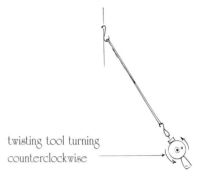

twisting tool turning counterclockwise

6. Tie both ends to secure and remove from the hook.

Triple & Quadruple Bullion Cord

This is worked just like the double bullion, but with three or four groups of yarns instead of two. A "tool" I like to use for making multiple bullion cords is the plate rack clamped to a table.

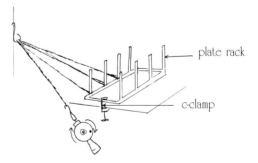

plate rack

c-clamp

You can make as many multiples of cording as you have pegs on one side of the rack. You could even put double or triple groups of twisted yarns on each peg since the wood is sticky enough and long enough to allow for this.

Fancy Wrapped Cording

Fancy wrapped cording.

If you are so inclined, you can wrap your own thick cord and use this "in the mix" for a very elaborate cord. This takes some time, but is mindless and can be done while you watch TV
.

1. Cut a 1/8″ or 3/16″ diameter piping cord (available at most fabric stores) to the desired length for the cording (remember it will probably be doubled for the finished cord).
2. With the thread or threads of your choice, secure at the end of the piping cord and twist the cord to wind the yarn or thread around the cording, completely covering it.
Note: This is an ideal way to use variegated yarn or thread, which makes a striped cord.

Fancy Beaded Cord

Seed beads threaded through cording.

If you plan to use beaded cording as you would most unbeaded cording (i.e., pulling it through the finial), this will be a bit more challenging than you may think. But let's think simple.

1. Use a beading needle or dental floss threader (my favorite beading needle) to thread relatively small beads on one of the lengths of yarn or thread you plan to use for the hanging cord.
2. Distribute the beads evenly across the yarn, then twist to create the bullion.
3. Beaded hanging cords don't work well for threading on the flounce disk or wheel or through the center

of the finial since the beads, no matter how small, often prevent this. You can use a plain yarn or thread, bring it up through the center of the finial, catch the beaded cord, and thread it back down the center of the finial, then knot the ends together.

Half-and-Half Bullion Cord

This hanging cord is made of half yarn and half silk ribbon.

This is basically the same as a single bullion cording but with two different types of yarn. It can also be made double, triple - whatever you wish. These instructions are for the single.

1. Determine how long a cord you want and calculate the yarn requirement for a one-color single bullion cord (see page 33). Divide that amount in half and cut equal lengths of yarn or thread.
2. Knot both ends securely to form a circle.
3. Twist to create the single bullion as you would ordinarily.

Other Cording Embellishments

Now that you have mastered the basics, try adding small silk flowers, unusual beads, thin metal chain - your options are endless. But, most of all, enjoy both the process and the results!

Chapter VI

Fabulous Fringe
Creating Drama & Elegance

Besides being the critical first step in tassel making, fringe making is an art unto itself. By focusing purely on creating interesting fringe, you are also providing yourself with the first step in creating interesting tassels. Fringe consists of two types: **cut-edge**, where the bottom edge of the fringe is plain yarn that has been cut, and **bullion**, where the yarn has been twisted and doubled back to create a series of rope-like lengths. Commercially, as it's woven and cut or bullioned, all fringe is simultaneously attached to trim or some type of stabilizing tape that is then sewn into the seams of pillows, edges of curtains, or other applications.

The fringe you make from the instructions in this book is secured with rows of machine or hand stitching. Whether or not you attach twill tape or woven trim is your choice, but is not critical to the application of the fringe to your project.

Fringe on Pillows

If you are already a sewer, you may choose to make your own pillow from fabric. If you are not a sewer, you may attach your fringe to a purchased pillow, although the application of the fringe will be different and will require either hand sewing or gluing. Some fabric glues are washable, dry clear, and are quite strong, so you may want to consider these options for embellishing a commercially made pillow, especially if it's an inexpensive one or one to be used only for special occasions.

Besides the obvious application of edging all around the edges or along two edges of a pillow, consider other embellishments such as diagonally across the front of a pillow or gathered together in the center of the a pillow.

By creating the fringe yourself, you can customize it by making it in varying lengths, making it double thickness with contrasting colors, adding beaded fringe (purchased or made by you), using unusual yarns, making it especially long or short - the possibilities are endless. Not only will you save money by making your own fringe, you can make it to match your decor. There are so many colors, textures, fibers, and thicknesses of yarn available (see Resources on page 128) that you will never have a problem making a fringe to coordinate with your color scheme, regardless of how unusual it may be.

Fringe on Lampshades & Accessories

The Victorian uses of embellishment is nowhere more dramatic than in the lampshades of the era. You can duplicate these elegant pieces with the use of cotton and/or rayon embroidery floss or thread and the addition of pearl or other drop beads at the ends of each piece of bullion fringe. By threading a jewelry end pin with a drop bead and forming a loop at the top of the pin, you can create your own custom beaded fringe.

Another very popular use for fringe in Victorian times was along the edge of a table scarf. This fringe was often thinner and more del-  icate, especially when used in conjunction with sheer or lightweight fabrics. Still other uses of fringe were for accents on decorative boxes, on flags, even along the edges of bookshelves - it seems wherever there was a surface, there was a use for fringe.

Fringe on Furniture

Oddly, one of the most popular uses of heavy bullion fringe was to protect expensive uphol-stery on chairs and sofas from the wear of boots and shoes kicking against the edge of the furniture. This practical use of fringe was, however, overshadowed by the rich and elegant appearance of the fringe on the upholstered chair or couch.

Another obvious application for fringe was around footstools, which often boasted fringe that complemented the fringe on the chair or sofa.

One of the most unusual and effective uses of fringe is on a headboard or canopy. Again, a rich, dramatic look is created with the addition of bullion fringe while a totally different feeling can be generated through the use of cut-edge fringe. Fringe edging on a bedskirt or bedspread makes a real statement.

Fringe on Window Treatments

Lastly, and most obviously, is the use of fringe in window treatments and ac-cents. By adding a rich bullion fringe to the edges of a simple cur-tain, the entire feeling and look of a room is dramatically changed. Fringe can be used on tiebacks, along curtain edges, on valances, on swags, along the edge of shades, and more.

There are many wonderful window treatment books available, to say nothing of the countless decorating magazines that can provide more than enough inspiration for exciting and innovative ways to use fringe as part of window accents.

Choosing the Yarn or Thread

When selecting a yarn for fringe, decide how you would like the fringe to appear: fuzzy, elegant, colorful, rustic, etc.

Just as there are casual rugs (Berber, raffia, etc.), there are yarns that work best with casual looks. These include cotton, linen, wool, and many blends. Likewise, for an elegant look try using silk, rayon (plied or chenille), mercerized cotton, or some blends.

The above are just suggestions - the ulti-mate appearance and application for fringe will be unique to the decorator. Just never eliminate any interesting application for fringe - there are no rules when it's your house!

Fringed Beaded Lampshade

The fringe on this lampshade is much easier to make than it may seem. The lampshade frame comes with all the instructions for applying fabric and trim - all you do is make the fringe. The pearl drop beads can be found in most jewelry supply catalogs and the end pins you can make during some "mindless" time (does the tube come to mind?).

I've included instructions for applying the fabric in case you decide to use a lampshade that is old or not intended for re-covering.

Difficulty rating:
Intermediate

Finished size of shade:
9-1/4″ high x 10″ around at fullest part

Finished length of fringe:
2-1/2″ including bead

Materials & Tools

- ✿ tulip lampshade frame
- ✿ paper for pattern
- ✿ pencil
- ✿ 1/2 yd. cream color fabric, 44″-54″ wide
- ✿ 2 packages cream color fold-over bias tape, 1/2″ wide
- ✿ 3 yds. braid, 3/8″ wide
- ✿ 5 skeins cream color rayon embroidery floss
- ✿ 5 skeins cream color cotton embroidery floss

- ✿ 144 pearl drop beads 6-8mm diameter*
- ✿ 144 end pins, 1-1/2″ long*
- ✿ double-faced tape, 1/4″ wide
- ✿ fabric glue
- ✿ round-nose jewelry pliers
- ✿ wire cutters
- ✿ beading needle or dental floss threader
- ✿ Tassel Master or crochet fork
- ✿ E-Z Twister (if not using Tassel Master)

*** You can purchase drop pearls with metal loops pre-inserted made by Darice (see Resources).**

Making the Shade

1. Draw the outline of each of the different lampshade panels onto the paper using the frame as a template. (*Most lampshade frames come with complete instructions for making a paper pattern.*) Cut out the pattern pieces from the paper, position the paper pattern pieces on the frame to test for size, then cut out panels from fabric, adding 1/2″ around all edges. Keeping the bias tape folded, wrap tape around all parts of the lampshade frame that will have the fabric panels attached.

2. Glue the panels of fabric to the shade frame. Trim the fabric so the raw edges of the fabric meet.

3. Glue braid along the six vertical panel lines, then around the top edge, then around the zigzag lower edge.

Making the Fringe

1. Insert an end pin through each bead from the bottom up. Cut off all but 1/4″ of the wire above the bead and make a loop using the round-nose pliers. Repeat for all beads.

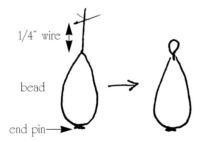

2. Split the floss so there are three plies of each type.

3. Hold one 3-strand length of each floss together and twist the floss on either the Spinning Spool (comes with the Tassel Master) or the E-Z Twister/Winder.

4. Using a beading needle or floss threader, thread 26 beads (through the loop you made on the top of each bead) onto the end of the twisted yarn.

5. If you are using Tassel Master, insert one row of pegs along Position #1 and one row along Position #2. If you are using a crochet fork, insert the bars so they are separated by 2″.

6. Following the instructions that come with Tassel Master, or, if you are using the crochet fork, tie the end of the twisted yarn to one bar and slide the beads along the twisted yarn, leaving a bead at the lower edge of each wrap across the fork. Be sure there are just 26 beads every 6-1/4″ (this is the measurement of the bottom edge of each lampshade panel).

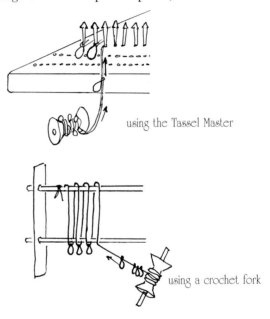

using the Tassel Master

using a crochet fork

7. Apply tape or stitch through the top and remove the yarn from the board or fork.

8. Apply a length of double-faced tape along the lower edge on the inside/wrong side of the fork, on the bias tape.

9. Remove the paper on the reverse side of the tape and apply the top edge of the fringe so it hangs down but the top is concealed.

10. Apply a bead of fabric glue along all raw edges of fabric, one section at a time, and apply 3/8″ braid. Work vertical sections first, then around the top of the shade, then along the lower edge.

wrong side

Oval Fringed Box

Boxes like this are ideal for holding useful items, which may not be appropriate or practical to display. Make one for each room in the house, changing the fabric and fringe color to match the decor. Use round, square, or hexagonal paper maché boxes. Add a tassel or two on the top. The options are endless!

Difficulty rating:
Intermediate

Finished size:
6″ x 9″ oval x 4″ high

Materials & Tools

- oval paper maché box, 6″ x 9″ oval x 4″ high
- 1/3 yd. upholstery fabric, 44″ wide
- 1 spool pale gold color chainette yarn or rayon cord
- 2 yds. gold metallic braid
- fabric glue
- double-faced tape
- spray adhesive
- removable masking tape
- fabric marking pencil
- Tassel Master, Tatool, or crochet fork

Covering the Lid

1. Place the lid upside down on the wrong side of the fabric and trace around the edge.

2. Cut out the oval, adding 1/2″.

3. Apply a coating of spray adhesive to the top of the lid.

4. Center the fabric on the box lid and glue it in place. Snip the seam allowance to go around the curve of the box lid, and glue the seam allowance to the side of the lid.

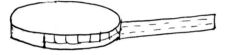

snip the seam allowance to fit the curve of the lid

5. Cut a strip of fabric 2″ x 25″. Fold in 1/2″ on both long raw edges and glue it to the edge of the lid, folding in and gluing the ends.

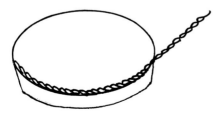

cover the snipped seam allowance with a fabric strip

Covering the Box

1. Cover the upper edge of the box that fits into the lid with removable masking tape.

2. Apply a coating of spray adhesive to the sides of the box. Let set. Remove the masking tape.

3. Cut a strip of fabric 4″ x 25″. Press in 1/2″ along upper edge and lightly glue to the wrong side. Adhere fabric around the sides of the box, folding in 1/2″ on both ends where the fabric meets at the back of the box.

4. Around the bottom of the box, snip the seam allowance as you did with the lid and glue it to the bottom of the box.

5. Cut a 15-foot length of chainette. Triple the yarn and tie the ends together to form a circle. Loop over a hook and twist tightly to make a 25″ long single bullion cord.

6. Glue the cord around the top edge of the box.

Making the Fringe & Trim

1. Holding two strands of chainette together, make a 25″ length of 1-1/2″ long bullion fringe.

If using the Tassel Master, insert a row of pegs in Position #1 and another row of pegs in Position #2. Holding two strands of chainette together, wrap the board. Apply double-faced tape and remove the lower pegs to release the bullion fringe.

If using the Tatool or crochet fork, wrap the frame with twisted chainette. Apply double-faced tape, remove from the tool, then stitch to secure.

2. Cut a 15-foot length of chainette. Triple the chainette and make two 25″ long single bullion cords in the same way you made the cord above.

3. Glue the upper edge of the 25″ length of fringe from Step 1 around the box 1/2″ from the top edge.

4. Glue one 25″ length of bullion cord from Step 2 around the edge of box just below where the lid will sit.

5. Glue two rows of gold metallic braid just above the bullion cording.

6. Glue a second length of bullion cord around the edge of the box, above the two rows of braid.

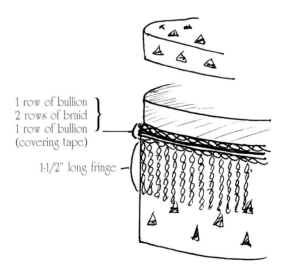

1 row of bullion
2 rows of braid
1 row of bullion
(covering tape)

1-1/2″ long fringe —

Fringed & Tasseled Christmas Stocking

S tockings are one of the best and most interesting templates for adding many types of embellishment, especially tassels and fringe. You can embellish a purchased stocking or one you've sewn yourself. By adding a few subtle touches, this undecorated upholstery weight purchased stocking became an ideal stocking for either a man or woman.

Difficulty rating:
Beginner to Intermediate

Finished length of tassel:
5″

Materials & Tools

- plain purchased stocking with folded-over edge
- 1 ball antique gold rayon crochet thread
- 1 ball light gold chainette*
- 1 skein antique gold cotton embroidery floss
- 1 yd. metallic gold braid, 1/8″ round

- fabric glue
- double-faced or removable tape
- Trim Tool, Tatool, or cardboard 5″ wide x any length
- Tassel Master or crochet fork
- yarn darner
- cardboard or plastic tube, 5/8″ diameter

If you use acetate chainette, be sure not to wash the stocking.

Making the Fringe & Cord Trim

Note: Apply a dot of fabric glue to all permanent knots, since rayon yarn/thread doesn't hold a knot well.

1. If using the Tassel Master, Tatool, or a crochet fork, set the tool for a length of 2-1/2″ (Positions #1 and #3 on the Tassel Master). Make bullion fringe by holding two strands of chainette and two strands of crochet thread together equal to the circumference of the cuff of the stocking plus 2″.

2. Remove the fringe from the board or frame and sew or glue it to the underside of the fold-over edge of the stocking. (*Note:* If you plan to wash or otherwise clean the stocking, do not use the double-faced tape as instructed in the Tassel Master directions. Use removable tape, stitch through the top of the fringe above the tape, then remove the tape.)

3. Make bullion cord #1 the same length as the fringe from one 2-yard strand of crochet thread and one 2-yard strand of chainette held together and tied to form a circle.

4. Make bullion cord #2 the same length as the fringe from three 2-yard strands of chainette held together and tied to form a circle.

5. Apply the cording using fabric glue, as shown in the illustration.

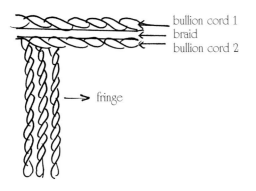

bullion cord 1
braid
bullion cord 2

fringe

Making the Tassel

1. Cut a 1-yard length of crochet thread and a 1-yard length of chainette to create the hanging cord for the tassel.

2. Double both yarns and, holding them together, tie the ends together to form a circle and knot securely. Apply a dot of glue to the knot.

3. Hang the unknotted loop over a hook and twist tightly. Bring the knotted end to the looped end, letting the yarn double back on itself. Knot the ends together to secure and apply a dot of glue to the knot. Do not knot into a circle.

4. Set the tassel-making tool of choice to 5″ or Position 5 on Tassel Master. Holding one strand of rayon crochet thread, wind the yarn around the tassel tool or piece of cardboard until 0approximately half the thread has been wound.

5. Tie a piece of cotton floss tightly at the top of the tassel to secure.

6. Thread the yarn darner with the loop end of the hanging cord from Step 1 through the top "eye" of the tassel.

7. If using a Trim Tool, tie a length of floss around the neck of the tassel to secure.

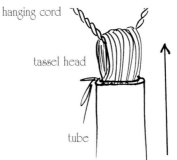

8. Cut the yarn evenly along the bottom end of the tassel to create a cut skirt.

9. Pull the hanging cord through the tube until 3/4″ of the tassel head appears. Tightly tie a double strand of embroidery floss around the tassel neck.

hanging cord

tassel head

tube

10. Remove the paper on the tape on the remaining 2″ of bullion fringe (from the fringe around the stocking itself) to expose the adhesive and wrap adhesive side in around the neck of the tassel.

11. Pull the tassel out of the tube. With a third "hand" holding the top of the tassel, wrap metallic braid around the tassel neck, starting at the top 1/2″ of the bullion fringe at the back of the tassel and winding toward the head of the tassel for 1/2″ or until there are four rows of braid.

12. Cut the braid at the back of the tassel and secure with glue.

13. Tie the hanging cord through the stocking's hanging loop.

Damask Stripe Pillow

This pillow is a super accent to any room and can easily be customized by just changing yarn and fabric.

Difficulty rating:
Beginner to intermediate

Finished size:
14″ x 14″

Materials & Tools

- ❋ 14″ pillow form
- ❋ 1/2 yd. cream color stripe damask fabric, 44″ wide
- ❋ 4 spools thin cream rayon cord, approximately twice the thickness of buttonhole twist thread
- ❋ 1 ball cream color mercerized crochet or tatting cotton
- ❋ Magicord Machine, spool knitter, hand knitting needles, or knitting machine
- ❋ Tassel Master, crochet fork, or Tatool

Making the Fringe

1. Holding one strand of the rayon and one of the cotton yarn together, use one of the I-cord knitting tools to make approximately 18 yards of knitted cording. (Refer to page 24 for instructions.) *Note:* The cording will be loosely knit and should be measured while stretched slightly.

2. If you are using Tassel Master, insert one row of pegs into Position #1 and one into Position #3. If you are using any of the other tools, set the tool or fork to 3″.

3. Loosely twist the knitted cording and wind it around the pegs or tool/fork. Release to create bullion.

4. Make 56″ of fringe, following the instructions that come with the tool.

Covering the Pillow

1. Cut one 14″ square of fabric for the pillow front and two 10″ x 14″ pieces for the back.

2. Fold under 1/2″ along one 14″ edge of both rectangular back pieces and sew.

3. Overlap the stitched edges by 3″ and baste along the overlapped edge. This piece should now measure 14″ square.

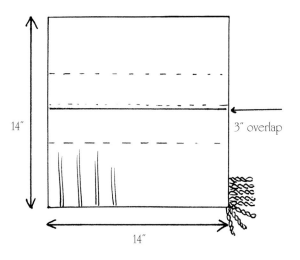

14″

3″ overlap

14″

4. Baste the top of the fringe around the edges of the 14″ square piece (either back or front) with the fringe facing to the center.

5. With right sides together, sew the front and back of the pillow together.

6. Trim the seams and turn right side out.

7. Insert the pillow form.

Floral Fantasy Footstool

This project was made from a punch needle embroidery kit, but you can use any fabric of your choice. The fringe was made from the same yarn used to punch the design and the tassels from the accent colors.

Difficulty rating:
Intermediate

Finished size:
13″ x 16″

Materials & Tools

* Floral Fantasy punch needle embroidery kit or 5/8 yd. upholstery fabric
* 13″ x 16″ piece of 1/2″ thick plywood with rounded edges
* 1/2 yd. cotton fabric (for lining and underside of footstool)
* foam, 13″ x 16″ x 2″ thick
* 5/8 yd. cotton batting
* 1-3/4 yds. black braid trim, 1/2″ or 3/4″ wide

* 10 100-yd. spools black punch embroidery yarn
* 1 spool each of 4 contrasting colors punch embroidery yarn
* 1 skein each of cotton embroidery floss colors to match the punch embroidery yarn colors
* tacky glue
* fabric glue
* masking tape

Covering the Footstool

Note: If you plan to work the punch design, do so first to measure 16″ x 18″. Instructions assume the punched design is complete. Leave 2″ to 3″ of extra fabric around all edges.

1. Glue the foam to the top of the footstool using tacky glue.

2. Wrap batting tightly around the foam and glue or staple it in place on the underside of the stool.

3. Center the punched design or fabric on the footstool top and pull tightly around all the edges. Staple it in place on the underside of the footstool. Or cut a piece of cotton fabric to

staple batting to bottom of stool top

wrap around the top and sides of the footstool top, and staple it to the edges of the underside of the footstool.

4. Cut another piece of fabric the dimensions of the underside of the footstool top plus 1″ around.

5. Press under 1″ around all edges and stitch (or glue) 3/4″ from the folded edge.

6. Glue the piece to the underside of the footstool top using fabric glue.

Making the Fringe

1. Knit all the black punch yarn on the Magicord Machine.

2. On the Tassel Master, insert pegs across Position #1 and Position #5, but keep one hole in every two empty.

3. Make bullion fringe by lightly twisting the knitted cord as you wind it around the pegs. Test the amount of twist since you want a soft (slight) twist.

4. Apply masking tape 1/4″ below the upper pegs and release the pegs at the lower edge to create fringe.

5. Zigzag stitch above the tape, then remove the tape.

6. Glue the fringe to the lower edge of the footstool top (or use the double-faced tape that comes with Tassel Master).

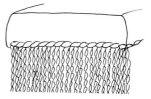

glue fringe along lower edge of footstool top

7. Apply the double-faced tape over the top of the fringe and apply the braid.

Making the Tassels

1. Make four 7″ long single bullion hanging cords from each of the four remaining colors of punch yarn by first cutting two 18″ lengths of yarn. Holding both strands together, knot to form a circle. Hang the looped end over a hook and twist. Bring the knotted end to the looped end and let the yarn double back on itself to create the bullion cording. Knot the ends to secure and set aside. Repeat for each of the remaining four colors.

2. Set the Trim Tool to 3″ and make four tassels, each in a different color. Follow the Trim Tool instructions for making a basic tassel and leave a 10″ length of floss at the top. (Wrap the tassels with punch yarn as low around the tassel neck as tightly as the tool will allow without breaking the yarn.)

3. Turn the basic tassels into "puff" or "squab" tassels by first pushing down the yarn wrapped around the neck of the tassel so it is 1-1/2″ below the tie at the top of the tassel.

4. Thread the floss at the top of the tassel with the tapestry needle and insert the needle through the center of the tassel, pushing the neck of the tassel up to create a "puff" effect.

5. Secure the floss at the wrapped neck and bring it back up through the center to the top of the tassel.

6. Using the tapestry needle, thread the unknotted end of the bullion cord through the "eye" at the top of the tassel and knot the ends to form a circle. Pull the knotted ends so they are hidden inside the eye of the tassel.

7. Sew a tassel to each of the four corners of the footstool, on top of the fringe.

Fringed Throw

By adding a fluffy bullion fringe to the edges of a soft but thick fabric, prefer-ably one with a texture, you can make an easy and colorful afghan to accent any room of your house as well as to use on cool evenings.

Making the Fringe

Note: You can make this throw as large or small as you wish.

1. Knit all the punch yarn on the Magicord Machine.

2. On the Tassel Master, insert pegs across Position #1 and Posi-tion #5, but leave one hole in every two empty.

3. Make bullion fringe by lightly twisting the knitted cord as you wind it around the pegs, making sure the twist is not very tight.

4. Apply removable masking tape 1/4″ below the upper pegs and release the pegs at the lower edge to create fringe.

5. Zigzag stitch above the tape, then remove the tape. Set the fringe aside while you prepare the fabric.

6. Trim the edges of the fabric to remove selvages and uneven cut edges.

7. Turn under 1/4″ and 1/4″ again to conceal the raw edge. Baste close to the fold.

8. Stitch the fringe close to the fold and again over the basting.

Difficulty rating:
Beginner

Finished size:
44″ x 60″

Materials & Tools

* 1-3/4 yds. textured fabric, 45″ wide
* 20 200-yd. spools acrylic punch embroidery yarn in coordinating color
* masking tape

* Magicord Machine
* Tassel Master
* sewing machine

Casbah Footstool

The appearance of the long fringe on this footstool reminded me of a fez, so the name "Casbah" was ideal. Since there is no true upholstery (no stapling or tacking), this project is easier than it looks. As with most projects in this book, you can use almost any type of yarn or thread as long as it hangs well.

Difficulty rating:
Intermediate

Finished size :
9″ x 12″ oval x 11″ high

Materials & Tools

- ❦ unfinished oval footstool, 9″ x 12″ oval x 11″ high
- ❦ 1/2 yd. upholstery fabric
- ❦ 1 spool cranberry chainette yarn or rayon cord
- ❦ 1 spool medium gold color chainette yarn or rayon cord
- ❦ 1″ diameter wood wheel with 1/4″ center hole
- ❦ thick foam rubber, 9″ x 12″ oval
- ❦ fabric glue
- ❦ spray adhesive

- ❦ wood dowel, 1/4″ diameter x 2″ long
- ❦ fabric marking pencil
- ❦ masking tape
- ❦ drill with 1/4″ bit
- ❦ cardboard, 8″ wide x 14″ long
- ❦ Tassel Master, Tatool, or crochet fork for bullion fringe
- ❦ Tassel Master with extension or cardboard 7-1/2″ x 14″ for cut edge fringe
- ❦ loop turner
- ❦ awl or thin steel knitting needle
- ❦ sewing machine

Making the Fabric Footstool Cover

1. Place the footstool upside down on the wrong side of the fabric and trace around the edge. Cut out, adding 3/4″ around all edges for a seam allowance.

2. Drill a hole through the center of the top of the wooden footstool.

3. Apply a coating of spray adhesive to the top of the footstool and affix the foam rubber oval.

4. Cut a strip of fabric 4-1/2″ x 36″ long. Sew the short ends together with a 3/4″ seam allowance to form a circle.

5. With right sides together, sew the fabric strip to the fabric oval, snipping the seam allowance to fit.

6. Turn under 1/2″ along the raw edge of the strip and sew 3/8″ from the fold.

Making the Fringe & Trim

1. Make 36″ of 7-1/2″ long cut edge fringe from the cranberry chainette. *Note:* You can make the fringe in separate sections for ease of handling.

If using the Tassel Master, insert a row of pegs in Position #1 on the upper board and Position #2 on the lower board. Holding two strands of cranberry chainette together, wrap the board to the desired thickness. Apply tape (if you plan to wash the footstool cover, apply removable masking tape 1/8″ below the normal tape position, then after removing the fringe from the board, zigzag stitch above the tape). Remove the lower pegs to release the fringe. Cut the lower loops.

If using cardboard, wrap the cardboard with cranberry chainette to the desired thickness, making sure the fringe is evenly spread across with none overlapping. On both sides of the cardboard, apply tape 1/4″ from the top of the cardboard, making sure each strand is adhered to the tape. Cut the lower loops to remove the fringe from the cardboard. Stitch through both thicknesses of yarn. Repeat until you have a 36″ length of fringe.

2. Make 36″ of 3-1/2″ long bullion fringe by holding two strands of gold chainette together.

If using the Tassel Master, insert a row of pegs along Position #1 and a second row along Position #4.

If using a crochet fork, adjust the fork to 4″. Refer to Step 1 for instructions for using tape and for stitching.

3. Baste the gold bullion fringe to the cranberry cut skirt fringe close to existing stitch lines. These stitch lines will later be covered by bullion cording trim.

4. Sew the doubled fringe to the inside edge of the top of the footstool cover.

5. Make four 36″ long single bullion cords as follows: make one triple strand and two double strands with cranberry, and one triple strand with gold.

6. Sew or glue the bullion cords just above the fringe on the outside of the footstool cover in the following sequence, from bottom to top: triple strand cranberry, triple strand gold, double strand cranberry, double strand cranberry.

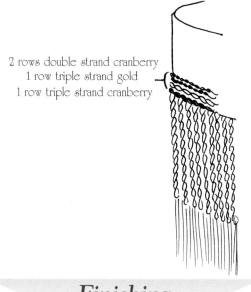

2 rows double strand cranberry
1 row triple strand gold
1 row triple strand cranberry

Finishing

1. Spray a coating of adhesive on the wood wheel and let set.

2. Yarn wrap the wheel (using the finial-covering technique) with cranberry chainette.

3. Cut a 2-yard length of cranberry chainette. Double it and knot to make a circle. Place the unknotted end over a hook and twist tightly. Bring the unknotted end to the knotted end and let the yarn double back on itself to create a bullion cord. Knot the ends securely to form a circle and apply a dot of glue to secure the knot.

4. Thread the wood wheel onto the bullion cording and push to knot.

5. Use the awl to make a hole in the center of the foam rubber and fabric cover, matching the hole that is drilled in the wood.

6. Insert the loop turner from the bottom of the footstool up to the top through the hole.

7. Insert the looped end of the bullion cording into the hook end of the loop turner and pull through to the bottom of the footstool. Pull the cording tightly so the wheel makes a slight depression in the top of the footstool.

8. Knot the ends of the bullion around the short dowel to hold it in place.

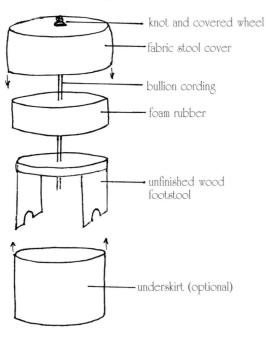

knot and covered wheel

fabric stool cover

bullion cording

foam rubber

unfinished wood footstool

underskirt (optional)

Making the Fabric
Underskirt (optional)

Make this underskirt to hide the legs of the footstool.

1. Cut out a 9″ x 32″ strip of the same fabric.

2. Turn under 1/2″ along both 32″ raw edges and stitch 3/8″ from the fold.

3. Circle the legs of the footstool with the fabric strip, pull snug, and pin.

4. Remove the fabric strip from the footstool and sew a seam along the 9″ raw edges where pinned. Trim the seam if necessary.

5. Slide the fabric onto the legs of the footstool under the fringe.

Chapter VII

Soft Tassels

Interesting Looks for Simple Tassels

Soft tassels are tassels without a finial top, usually made by winding yarn around one of the tools described in Chapter III. They are also used as overskirts, embellishments on finial tassels, or in groups to make one large tassel. This chapter explores these simply-made tassels and focuses on how you can easily embellish them for a unique look.

To make soft tassels, you'll need sharp scissors (sewing and embroidery types), fabric glue, one of the tools mentioned in Chapter III, a tapestry needle, and a cardboard or plastic tube the approximate diameter of the tassel. You can find an appropriate tube as the cardboard core holding elastic thread, Multi's Embellishment Yarn, ribbon floss, punch yarn - or you can find similar sizes in plastic piping at a hardware or plumbing supply store. They are usually from 1/2″ to 3/4″ in diameter.

cotton, trim, ribbon, etc. You can also make narrow bullion cording from regular sewing thread or a couple strands of 6-strand embroidery floss to wrap around the tassel.

After you have wound the yarn on the chosen tool and are ready to remove it, be sure to tie the top tightly with a cotton yarn, leaving at least 6″-long ends. You can tie the neck of the tassel now or after you use the tube tool.

1. Draw the ends tied to the top of the tassel through the tube until just the head of the tassel has been pulled out. The head can be whatever length you want.

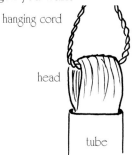

hanging cord

head

tube

Yarn Wrapping

Yarn wrapping is the technique of wrapping yarn or cording around the head or neck of the tassel for decorative as well as practical reasons (such as holding the tassel together). Gimp is an all-time favorite wrapping material and is used extensively in commercially-made tassels, but you can use many types of cording or yarn including embroidery floss, perle

Yarn wrapping is both decorative and functional.

2. Tie a length of cotton yarn or floss tightly around the neck of the tassel (just under the head), leaving a 3″ length of the floss to tuck in later.

3. Wrap the head or neck. The tube makes the tassel easy to handle, especially for slippery tassels made from

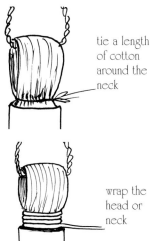

tie a length of cotton around the neck

wrap the head or neck

rayon threads. Before you wrap the neck of the tassel, be sure to thread the cotton floss or yarn you used to initially tie the tassel or you can apply a dot of fabric glue to the knot and snip off the yarn or floss close to the knot.

4. Using this method, you can attach beads or other embellishments quite easily.

Netting

Netting can be used for both soft tassels or finial-topped tassels. With this technique, you create a netted cap that slides over or is worked on the head of a soft tassel or on all or a portion of a finial-topped tassel. The net serves as a decorative touch while coordinating (or contrasting) the finial with the skirt.

Netting can be done with coordinating or contrasting color threads.

There are basically two different types of netting: 1) a version of the buttonhole stitch often called "catch stitch" (also called "detached buttonhole stitch"), or 2) knotting, as for macramé.

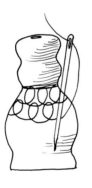

There are advantages and disadvantages of both techniques, although both are easy and effective. The catch stitch is quicker and uses just one strand of thread, but it is more challenging to introduce beads into the design. The macramé technique is a bit easier to control and can include beads into the netted design, but it is a bit more time-consuming and requires the use of more than one strand of yarn. See page 66 for more information on netting.

The easiest method for creating a catch-stitch net for the head of a soft tassel is to execute it on the same tube as described in Yarn Wrapping, but as a second step after the hanging cord has been attached to the tassel head. Some people prefer to work the netting on a dowel, but I've found it difficult to slide the net-

ting off the dowel and onto the head of the tassel. By working the netting on the tube, you can use the hanging cord to pull the tassel up through the tube, then slide the finished, netted cap over the head as it emerges.

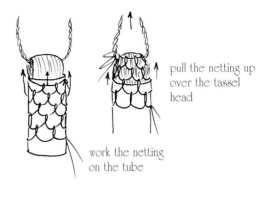

pull the netting up over the tassel head

work the netting on the tube

Beading

One of the best ways to embellish soft tassels is with beading. The size of the beads is determined by the size of the tassel, obviously, but imagination is really the key. Since I also enjoy jewelry-making, adding beads to tassels is a natural and can make the difference between a plain, boring tassel and a truly unique one.

Example of beaded embellishment on soft tassel.

There are so many ways to add beads to your tassels, I couldn't possibly cover them all here. Many of the projects in this book feature added beading. Refer to the individual project instructions to learn how to do it.

Basic Cage-Top Yarn Tassel

This is a very easy yet impressive tassel that can be easily embellished for special occasions. The netting makes the tassel stand out from more plain yarn tassels.

Difficulty rating:
Beginner

Finished size:
Small tassel - 3-1/2″
Large tassel - 6″

Materials & Tools

Small tassel
✱ 2 skeins perle #5 cotton yarn - 1 dark blue, 1 rose pink
✱ sturdy cardboard, 3-1/2″ wide x 4″-5″ long
✱ cardboard or plastic spool with 1/2″ diameter center hole
✱ tapestry needle

Large tassel
✱ 2 spools (80 yds.) Multi's Embellishment Yarn in Holiday color (or other cotton/rayon yarn)
✱ 1 skein perle #5 cotton - deep red
✱ 1 spool metallic yarn - deep red
✱ sturdy cardboard, 6″ x any length, or folding hat rack (that can fold to 6″ between pegs)
✱ cardboard or plastic spool with 3/4″ center hole
✱ tapestry needle

Making the Small Tassel (Blue)

1. Cut a 36″ length of each color of perle #5. Double them and knot to form a circle.
2. Twist to make a single bullion hanging cord. Knot to form a circle.
3. Cut a 10″ length of blue perle #5 and lay it across the top of the cardboard. Wrap the rest of the blue perle #5 around the cardboard over the 10″ length as shown.

lay the 10″ length on top of the cardboard

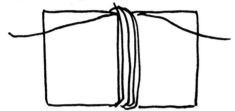

wrap the rest of the yarn around the cardboard

4. Remove the yarn from the cardboard and set the tassel aside.
5. Use rose perle #5 to make netting on a tube (see page 53).
6. Thread the tapestry needle with the floss securing the top of the tassel and insert it into the tube from the bottom through the top, pulling the tassel up.
7. When the top of the tassel has begun to emerge, slide the netting off the tube onto the head of the tassel and tighten. Continue drawing the tassel through the tube.
8. Tie the netting at the tassel neck. Thread the tapestry needle with the yarn ends and weave them into the tassel to hide.
9. Catch the center of the bullion cording with the 10″ length of blue perle #5 tied around the top of the tassel and knot securely.
10. Thread the ends of the blue perle #5 back into the tassel.
11. Cut the lower edge of the tassel.

Making the Large Tassel

1. Cut a 2-yard length each of red perle #5 and Multi's. Double them and knot to form a circle.
2. Twist to make a single bullion hanging cord. Knot to form a circle.
3. Cut a 10″ length and a 2-yard length of deep red perle #5. Set the 2-yard length aside to use for netting. Lay the 10″ length across the top of the cardboard as before.
4. Wrap the remaining deep red perle #5, one strand of deep red metallic, and two strands of Multi's around the cardboard or the hat rack pegs until one full skein of the perle cotton is used entirely. Continue winding with Multi's and metallic yarn until the Multi's spool is either used up or until you've reached the desired thickness of tassel. Remove the tassel from the cardboard or hat rack.
5. Tighten the 10″ length of deep red perle #5 at the top of the tassel, making sure both ends are equal in length. Set the tassel aside.
6. Use the 2-yard length of perle cotton to make netting on a tube as described on page 53.
7. Insert the tapestry needle threaded with the yarn tied at the top of the tassel from the bottom of the tube through the top, pulling the tassel up. When the top of the tassel has begun to emerge, slide the netting off the tube onto the head of the tassel and tighten. Continue drawing the tassel through the tube.
8. Tie the netting around the tassel neck and weave the ends to the inside of the tassel.
9. Catch the center of the bullion cording with the 10″ length of perle #5 tied around the top of the tassel and knot securely.
10. Cut the lower edge of the tassel.

Table Scarf Tassel

This easy-to-make tassel can have numerous decorative applications. Use it to accent a table, drape from the base of a candle, accent a picture frame, personalize a computer monitor, wear as a pendant, accent an evening purse …

Difficulty rating:
Beginner

Finished length:
3″

Materials & Tools

- 1 spool Multi's Embellishment Yarn in Woodlands color
- 4 pale green cut-glass teardrop beads, 5/8″ long
- 16 small, pale green cut-glass disk-shaped beads
- various small, pale green cut-glass beads

- fabric glue
- yarn darner
- loop turner
- beading needle and thread
- Trim Tool or sturdy cardboard, 3″ wide x 4″- 5″ long

Making the Tassel

1. Cut one 36″ length of Multi's and twist it tightly to make a single bullion cord. Knot the yarn to form a circle. Hang the looped end over a hook and twist. Bring the knotted end to the looped end and let the yarn double back on itself to create the bullion cording. Knot the ends to secure and set aside.

2. Set the Trim Tool to make a 3″ tassel and wrap the Multi's yarn around the tool to the desired thickness. Or wrap the yarn around the cardboard to the desired thickness.

3. Cut a 10″ length of cotton floss and thread it in the eye of a yarn darner. Draw it through the top of the tool under the head of the tassel. Tie securely. If you are using the cardboard, lay the 10″ length of floss on top of the cardboard and wrap the cardboard to the desired thickness for the tassel. Tie the floss tightly and remove from the cardboard.

4. Thread the eye of the yarn darner with the unknotted end of the bullion cord and draw it through the top of the tool under the head of the tassel. If you are using the cardboard, thread the bullion cord through the head of the tassel.

5. Open up the folded end of the bullion cord and thread it through the knotted end of the cording.

6. Cut a 12″ length of Multi's and wrap it once around the neck of the tassel and knot.

7. Cut the bottom end of the tassel and remove it from the tool or cardboard.

8. Tighten the Multi's at the top of the tassel and apply a dot of glue to the knot. Snip off the excess and push the knot to the inside of the tassel.

9. Wrap Multi's ten times (approx. 3/8″) around the neck of the tassel, tighten, and knot. Apply a dot of glue to the knot and snip off the ends.

10. Cut two 12″ lengths of the thread and thread on beads, following the arrows in the illustration.

11. Make two lengths of beads separated by a 1/2″ length of thread. Set aside.

12. Tie a separate length of thread around the neck of the tassel just under the wrapped neck. Thread this behind the wrapped neck and up through the top. Thread on three medium sized green beads and catch the two beaded lengths in the center 1/2″ and secure with a knot to the thread tied around the lower edge of the wrap around the tassel neck.

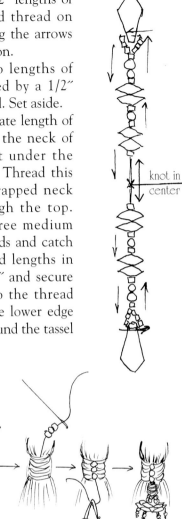

knot in center

13. Cut off an 8″ length of Multi's and wrap it around the 1/2″ thread holding the beaded strands to the lower edge of the tassel neck. Secure by tying in back and adding a drop of glue. Snip off the excess Multi's.

14. Cut two 24″ lengths of two strands of Multi's, knot to form a circle, and twist to create a bullion hanging cord.

15. Double the hanging cord and, using a loop turner, thread the folded end through the top "eye" of the tassel. Knot the doubled cord to form a circle.

Green 'n Gold

This tassel is meant to show that there is more to making soft tassels than wrapping and tying. You can add almost as many embellishments to a soft tassel as you can to a finial-topped tassel. The beading is fun and you can make the tassel any size you wish.

Difficulty rating:
Beginner to Intermediate

Finished length:
7″

Materials & Tools

- ❀ 1 ball (100 yds.) antique gold rayon crochet cotton thread
- ❀ 6 yds. olive color gimp
- ❀ 24″ length of any color cotton embroidery floss
- ❀ 36 glass beads in six graduating sizes (2mm-6mm) and colors
- ❀ fabric glue
- ❀ sturdy cardboard, 7″ wide x any length
- ❀ beading needle
- ❀ cardboard or plastic tube, 3/4″ diameter

Making the Tassel

Note: Rayon crochet thread has a "mind of its own," meaning it is very slippery and a knot made in this yarn will not stay tied, so keep this in mind as you work. This is where the tube helps to control the threads and why the tassel must be secured with cotton threads or floss.

1. Cut one 36″ length of gimp to make one of the bullion hanging cords.

2. Bring the ends together to form a circle and knot securely. Hang the looped end of the circle over a hook and twist tightly. Bring the knotted end to the looped end, letting the yarn double back on itself. Knot the ends together to secure. Do not knot into a circle.

3. Cut two 36″ lengths of rayon crochet thread to create another bullion hanging cord. Repeat Step 2.

4. Wrap the crochet thread around the cardboard until the entire ball has been used.

5. Cut off a 12″ length of the floss and double it. Thread it and the two bullion hanging cords through the top of the tassel.

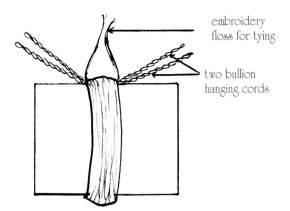

embroidery floss for tying

two bullion hanging cords

6. Tie the floss threaded through the top of the tassel tightly to secure temporarily and remove from the cardboard.

7. Holding the bullion hanging cord, pull the tassel into the tube until 1/2″ of the tassel head extends above the tube.

8. Cut the bottom edges of the yarn evenly along the opposite end of the tassel.

9. Tie a length of floss around the neck of the tassel to secure. Make 14 wraps of gimp around the tassel neck. Tie to secure and thread the ends into the tassel to hide.

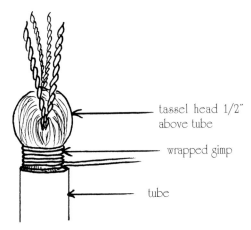

tassel head 1/2″ above tube

wrapped gimp

tube

10. Make one 18″ long bullion cord from the remaining gimp (refer to Step 2).

11. Using invisible thread, sew the gimp bullion cord to the wrapped gimp around the tassel neck as follows: alternate and evenly space around the neck - 2″ loop, 1″ long loop, 2″ loop, 1″ loop, 2″ loop, and 1″ loop.

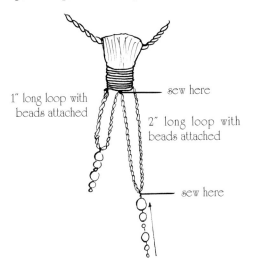

1″ long loop with beads attached

sew here

2″ long loop with beads attached

sew here

12. Using invisible thread, thread beads in descending size and affix to the lower edge of each gimp bullion loop.

Corded Footstool Slipcover

By adding an interesting slipcover over a purchased or old footstool, you can make an easy but dramatic change with just a yard of fabric, four easy-to-make tassels, and a bit of cording.

Difficulty rating:
Beginner to Intermediate

Finished size:
11″ x 16″ x 9″ high

Materials & Tools

- ❋ footstool, 11″ x 16″ x 9″ high
- ❋ 1 yd. plum upholstery fabric, 54″ wide
- ❋ 1 spool medium gold chainette yarn or rayon cord
- ❋ 1 skein gold cotton embroidery floss
- ❋ 1 skein gold metallic embroidery floss
- ❋ 1/4 yd. gold metallic trim, 1/2″ wide

- ❋ plum sewing thread
- ❋ fabric glue
- ❋ optional underskirt: 1/2 yd. coordinating or contrasting fabric
- ❋ fabric marking pencil
- ❋ accordion hat rack with minimum of 4 sets of 2 pegs
- ❋ sewing machine

Making the Tassel

Note: Make four 5″ long tassels.

1. Open the accordion rack so the pegs measure 10″ apart (measured from the center of the pegs).

2. Wind the chainette to the desired thickness around four sets of pegs to make four tassels.

3. Leaving a 6″ end, tie a piece of cotton floss securely around all the wound floss strands between the pegs.

4. Stretch out the rack to release the tassels.

5. Tie a length of cotton floss around each tassel neck to secure. Place a drop of glue on the knot and trim off the ends.

6. Cut a length of 1/2″ wide trim to fit around the neck of the tassel, over the floss. Glue the trim around the neck, positioning the seam on the back of the tassel.

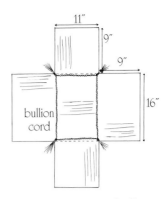

4. Turn in 3/4″ hems around all raw edges and stitch 1/2″ from the fold.

5. Place the slipcover on top of the stool so each side flap hangs evenly.

6. Separate the whole metallic floss skein into three 2-strand sections.

7. To make a 54″ long bullion cord, cut three 8-yard lengths of chainette and one 8-yard length of 2-strands of the metallic floss. Hold the chainette and floss together and hang the center of the combined strand over a hook. Twist, letting the yarn double back on itself to create bullion cord. Knot the end.

8. Sew or glue the bullion cord around the center top of the slipcover (refer to the illustration).

9. Sew a tassel at each corner.

Making the Slipcover

Note: If your footstool is a different size than mine, adjust the pattern measurements to fit your stool. All seam allowances and hems are 3/4″ wide. Finish all raw edges with an overcast or zigzag stitch.

1. Cut one 17-1/2″ x 30-1/2″ piece of fabric for the top and two wide sides of the slipcover.

2. Cut two 10-1/2″ x 12-1/2″ pieces of fabric for the two narrower sides, noting the placement and nap if you are using corded fabric.

3. With right sides together, center one side piece along the side edge of the center piece and sew the seam. Repeat for the opposite side.

Making the Underskirt (optional)

1. Measure the height of the foolstool legs and transfer this measurement to the underskirt fabric, adding 1-1/2″.

2. Cut the fabric to size and turn under 3/4″ along both raw edges and stitch 1/2″ from the fold.

3. Fit snugly around the legs of the footstool and pin.

4. Remove from the footstool and sew the seam along the raw edges where pinned. Trim the seam if necessary.

5. Slide the underskirt onto the legs of the footstool.

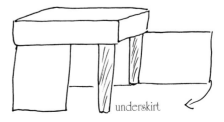

underskirt

Bridal Duet

Garter Tassel

Difficulty rating:
Beginner

Finished length:
2-1/4″

Ring Bearer Pillow

Difficulty rating:
Beginner to Intermediate

Finished length:
8″ square

Materials & Tools

Garter Tassel
* Purchased cream color garter with lace trim
* 1/4 yd. 1/8″ wide satin ribbon with small ribbon roses and leaves attached
* 1 skein cream color rayon embroidery floss
* 1 skein cream color cotton embroidery floss
* fabric glue
* Trim Tool or cardboard 2-1/2″ wide x any length
* chenille needle

Ring Bearer Pillow
* 1/4 yd. lightweight cream jacquard fabric
* 1/4 yd. cream cotton velveteen fabric

* 8″ square mini pillow form or polyester fiberfill
* 3 skeins cream color rayon embroidery floss
* 3 skeins cream color cotton embroidery floss
* 1/4 yd. cream braid with mini pearl beads, 1/2″ wide
* 1 yd. picot edge cream satin ribbon, 1/4″ wide
* 4 small ribbon roses with ribbon leaves
* cream sewing thread
* fabric glue
* Trim Tool
* chenille needle
* sewing thread to match fabric
* sewing machine
* fabric marking pencil

Garter Tassel

Add your own accent to this traditional wedding garter. Three small tassels make a purchased garter truly special. It coordinates with the Ring Bearer Pillow pictured and the Bridal Tassel (page 88) for a complete set.

Making the Tassel

Note: Make three tassels. These instructions are for one tassel.

1. Wrap the cardboard or Trim Tool 22 times with one 6-strand length each of rayon and cotton embroidery floss.

2. If you are using the Trim Tool, tie the neck of the tassel with cotton floss to secure, following the instructions that come with the tool.

3. Cut a 10″ length of cotton floss and thread it through the head of the tassel. If you are using the cardboard, thread a 6″ length of floss through the top of the tassel between the yarn and the cardboard and secure.

4. Cut the bottom edge loops and remove the tassel from the cardboard or Trim Tool.

5. Cut the ribbon trim so there is 1/2″ of ribbon on each side of one rose. (There is approximately 1″ of ribbon separating the roses.) Glue the trim around the neck of the tassel, overlapping the ribbon ends.

6. Thread the cotton floss on top of the tassel into a chenille needle.

7. Mark the front of the garter for attaching the tassels on the top, center, and lower edges, separated by 3/4″.

3/4″

8. Sew the tassels to the garter, tying off on the wrong side. Apply a dot of glue over the knot on the wrong side.

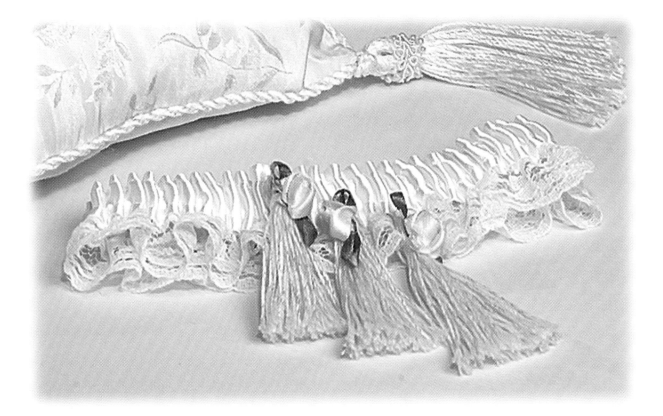

Ring Bearer Pillow

Make your special occasion even more special with the addition of elegant tassels that will coordinate all your wedding accent pieces. Because you've made it yourself, it will be that much more important to you in the years to come.

Making the Tassel

Note: Make four tassels. These instructions are for one tasssel.

1. Set the Trim Tool to make a 3-1/2″ tassel and wrap 15 times with one 6-strand length each of rayon and cotton embroidery floss.

2. Tie the neck of the tassel with cotton floss to secure.

3. Cut a 10″ length of cotton floss and thread it through the head of the tassel.

4. Cut the bottom edge loops of the floss and remove the tassel from the Trim Tool.

5. Cut a length of braid long enough to circle the neck of the tassel and glue it on the wrong side of the tassel to secure.

Making the Pillow

1. Cut a 9″ square each from jacquard and velveteen fabric.

2. On the jacquard fabric, measure 2″ from each cut edge and lightly mark a square.

3. Glue or stitch the satin ribbon along the marked lines, twisting at each corner to form a decorative loop. Glue or stitch a ribbon rose to each corner inside the loops.

4. With right sides together, sew three sides of the jacquard and velvet with a 1/2″ seam allowance.

5. Insert the pillow form or stuff with polyfil. Slip stitch the fourth side opening closed.

6. Cut one 3-yard length each of the 6-strand cotton and rayon embroidery floss.

7. Hold together one each of the 3-yard lengths of cotton and rayon floss and tie the ends together to form a circle.

8. Hang the loop end of the circle over a hook and twist tightly. Bring the knotted end to the looped end, letting the floss double on itself to create bullion. Knot the end to secure. You should have a length of bullion cording long enough to go around all four sides of the pillow, approximately one yard.

9. Sew or glue the bullion over the seam around the sides of the pillow.

10. Sew one tassel to each corner of the pillow, just above the bullion trim.

11. Cut 36″ lengths each of cotton and rayon floss and separate them into two 3-strand lengths.

12. Make 12″ long bullion cord for holding the rings by holding the rayon and cotton floss together and knotting the ends together to form a circle. Twist the floss tightly to create bullion.

13. With regular sewing thread, sew the center of the bullion cord to the center of the pillow and tack the pillow form inside.

14. Thread the wedding rings onto the center bullion cord and tie in a secure bow.

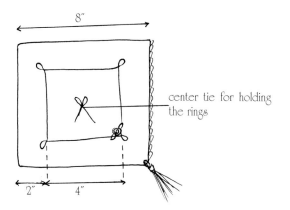

8″

center tie for holding the rings

2″ 4″

Chapter VIII

Terrific Finial Tassels
Topping It All Off

Tassels with finials are some of the most exciting to make since your imagination can literally go wild. The best ideas come from just keeping your eyes and mind open when reading home decorating books, visiting a craft store, or thinking before you discard an empty container.

Create one or two traditional designs, then branch out. I've used finials created from paper maché vegetables and fruit, small wood birdhouses sold in craft stores, mini ceramic pots with dried or silk flowers on top - let your mind be as creative as possible. Keep a small sketch pad with you when you travel or shop. Jot down ideas and impressions for translating items into fanciful tassels when you return home.

You can easily combine the techniques used in the tassels in this chapter to create your own design. Your imagination and the inexpensive shapes listed not only make your projects particularly interesting but can serve as the perfect rationalization for purchasing more expensive yarns for the tassel skirt.

The list below ranges from traditional finials to those you'd never imagine:

❀ Traditional tassel finials made from wood available in craft stores.

❀ Very large to medium sized finials from DIY (do-it-yourself) centers that were meant to be used on the top of a newel post.

❀ Mini-finials meant for use on dowels for hanging needlework projects.

❀ Wood parts of many types that can be found at most craft stores.

❀ Small cup-shaped containers including chair-leg caps.

❀ Christmas tree ornaments, napkin rings, candle decorations, etc.

❀ Corks, decorative drawer pulls, curtain rod finials, large-holed beads, pressed foam shapes, plumbing parts, etc.

❀ Discarded cap shapes such as the tops of jars, deodorant tops, 35mm film canisters, lipstick caps, spice jars, etc.

You should have the same basic tools on hand as described for the Soft Tassels (page 52) but with the addition of a chopstick or knitting needle, a threading wire, and double-faced tape.

Yarn Wrapping the Finial

This technique involves wrapping the finial, or part of the finial, with yarn, covering the raw material of the base. Gimp or other thin cording is an all-time favorite and used extensively in commercially-made tassels, but you can use nearly any type of cording or yarn. Using one of the twisting tools and regular sewing thread or a couple strands of 6-strand embroidery floss makes for exceptional cording to use for yarn wrapping.

1. Insert a chopstick or old knitting needle (one that's larger than the hole in the finial) into the bottom of the finial.

2. Spray the finial with a heavy coat of spray adhesive.

3. Insert the chopstick or knitting needle into a holder.

4. Hold and turn the chopstick or knitting needle while you affix the gimp or other yarn, making sure you keep the strands of yarn or cording close to each other to avoid gaps. It is best to wrap the finial from the narrowest to the thickest part. You may want to cut the yarn when the finial starts to narrow, then work from the bottom up, winding in the opposite direction to ensure the yarns will "meet" at the same point.

5. Tuck the ends inside the top and lower edge of the finial and apply a dot of glue to secure. Try not to handle the finials extensively since the threads can dislodge.

Netting on the Finial

As explained on page 53, there are basically two different types of netting. The first is a version of the buttonhole stitch also called a "catch stitch" and the second is knotting. Both techniques are easy and effective.

The knotting (macramé) technique is a bit easier to control, especially if you are working on a painted, not yarn-wrapped, finial, and can include beads into the netted design, but it is a bit more time-consuming and requires the use of more than one strand of yarn. Refer to page 100 for instructions on how to do knotting.

Netting made with the knotting technique.

It's easiest to do catch-stitch netting on a finial that has already been covered by gimp, cording, or yarn. The wrapped yarn helps keep the netting in position. Refer to page 53 for instructions on catch-stitch netting. Once you have mastered netting on a yarn-wrapped finial, try it on a painted finial. This creates a truly custom look without a great amount of time invested.

Catch-stitch netting.

Other Embellishing Methods

Try using some of the following ideas for decorating your finials. While I used some of them, there are always more ideas than there is time in the day. Please know this is only a partial list.

❁ Sponge painting
❁ Rubber stamping (use small stamps)
❁ Stenciling (use small stencils)
❁ Verdigris
❁ Covering with polymer clay slices
❁ Covering with polymer clay and adding pressed-in objects
❁ Bead wrapping
❁ Mosaics
❁ Dry or silk flowers

Applying Adhesive

Spray the finial with a heavy layer of spray adhesive. Alternatively, you can use thick tacky glue but it must be done in sections to keep the glue from drying before the embellishment material is applied since this type of glue tends to dry quickly.

Painting

It is advisable to paint all wood finials or parts with a base layer of gesso to allow for maximum color adhering.

Ruffs

The tassels we think of most when the image of an elaborate tassel comes to mind is one with a ruff, the usually fluffy embellishment that circles the lower edge of a finial-topped tassel. This embellishment not only provides a decorative touch but provides for the visual and often practical function of joining the finial top to the skirt.

This ruff was made by wrapping chenille stems around a knitting needle then wrapping the curled ruff around the lower edge of a decorated thread spool.

Traditional finials have a lip or lower edge where you can attach both the tassel skirt and, over it, a ruff to hide the wire most often used to attach a tassel skirt. In the past, ruffs have been one of the most time-consuming parts of the tassel to make, requiring the winding of wire around bunches of unruly yarn. Not for me, so I had to figure out some faster and easier methods. Detailed instructions for creating ruffs are given in each project that features the technique, but here are a few additional ideas.

❀ Use covered stem wire, preferably in white, and a marker or paint to color the covering. Then twist the wire into a flower shape and wire or glue it to the finial or make multiples for use as a ruff. The embellishment on the top of the Key tassel on page 84 was made this way.

❀ If using uncovered stem wire, apply a layer of spray adhesive to the wire, then wrap it with embroidery floss and bend similar to the painted wire above.

❀ Make punch needle flowers by punching three to four rings in different lengths and colors around a small circle. Apply fabric glue to the wrong side, let dry, and cut out. Apply to the finial or make multiple flowers to use as a ruff.

❀ Make ribbon roses by pulling one of the wired edges of wire-edge ribbon to form a circle. Glue this around the lower edge of the finial.

❀ My favorite idea is to use a chenille stem wrapped around a knitting needle as a ruff. Try holding two different colors together for a two-toned ruff.

❀ When using the Tassel Master, apply the tape 1/4˝ lower than normal. Wrap the skirt around the lower edge of the finial and secure tightly with wire. Then cut through the loops at the top of the skirt. This will create a look simulating a real ruff.

Southwestern

*A*lthough *this tassel may look quite complicated at first glance, it is actually quite easy. The finial is made from the leg for a footstool, which can be found at most home or lumber centers, punch embroidery yarn (you can also use crewel yarn or thin knitting machine yarn), and embroidery floss.*

Difficulty rating:
Intermediate

**Finished length
(excluding hanging cords):**
7-1/2″ including bead

Materials & Tools

- ❀ 3-3/4″ long (1-1/2″ diameter at fullest end) unfinished turned wood footstool leg
- ❀ oval wood bead, 2″ long
- ❀ acrylic paint: dusty rose, blue, yellow, green, yellow
- ❀ black fine-tip permanent marker
- ❀ matte finish glaze
- ❀ 2 (100-yd.) spools each of dusty rose, blue, yellow, green, and cream acrylic punch embroidery yarn
- ❀ 1 skein each dusty rose, blue, yellow, green, and cream cotton embroidery floss
- ❀ double-faced highly adhesive tape, 1/4″ wide
- ❀ fabric glue
- ❀ paintbrush

- ❀ weavers cloth (or other plain cotton/polyester blend fabric) the size to fit in hoop, plus 4″
- ❀ hand-held drill with 1/4″ bit
- ❀ vice
- ❀ pliers (if stool leg has screw end)
- ❀ umbrella swift or jig
- ❀ threading wire
- ❀ 4 Spinning Spools or dowel inserted into empty thread spool
- ❀ Tassel Master
- ❀ metal ruler
- ❀ double clip holder (optional)
- ❀ punch embroidery needle
- ❀ lock-lip embroidery hoop

Preparing the Finial

1. Remove the screw from the top of the wooden stool leg.

2. Drill a hole through the length of the leg, from top to bottom. (You will probably have to drill from both ends to complete the hole.)

3. Refer to the illustration to paint the wooden leg (finial) and let dry.

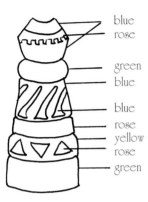

blue
rose

green
blue

blue
rose
yellow
rose
green

4. Paint the bead rose. Let dry.

5. Use the black marker to outline each separation of color on the finial.

6. Apply a coat of glaze to the finial and bead. Let dry.

Making the Tassel Skirt

1. Open the umbrella swift to a 16″ diameter (it will compact a bit as you wind the yarn on) or if using a jig, to a length of approximately 42″.

2. Hold two strands of the same color of punch yarn together and wind it around the swift or jig until there is only 1/4 of each spool remaining.

3. Using a double strand of punch yarn, tie at 3-1/2″ sections around the yarn in 11 places.

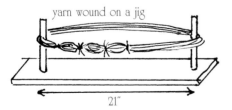

yarn wound on a jig

21″

4. Remove the yarn from the swift or jig.

5. Repeat this process for all the yarn colors. Do a final wrap with a combination of all the yarn colors except cream.

6. Cut the tied yarn into mini-tassel lengths by cutting through all lengths evenly spaced between the ties.

cut between the ties

7. On the Tassel Master, place a row of pegs along Position #1 and a second row along Position #2, but only fill every other hole along Position #2.

8. On the Spinning Spools, twist each color of floss separately. If you don't have four Spinning Spools and don't want to twist each color of floss separately, you can make your own Spinning Spools by inserting a length of dowel into an empty thread spool and sliding on a rubber band to hold the dowel in place.

9. Refer to the illustration and tie blue twisted floss to the first peg on Position #1. Wrap to the first peg on Position #2, but fold over one group of contrasting color yarn bunch. Use the ruler to hold down the yarn bunches as you work across the board.

10. Bring the twisted floss up between the first and second pegs on Position #1. Skip four pegs.

11. Repeat winding and adding the yarn bunch on the next peg (Steps 7 through 11). Tie off at the end.

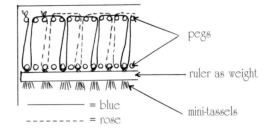

pegs

ruler as weight

_____ = blue
- - - - - - - - = rose

mini-tassels

12. Tie rose floss to the third peg on Position #1 and repeat the winding and adding of mini-tassel yarn as for the previous color. Be sure to use a contrasting color mini-tassel yarn.

13. Repeat Step 11 with the green and blue twisted floss. Use the floss color of your choice when adding the multi-color mini-tassel yarn.

14. Affix the tape 1″ below the pegs on Position #1 (halfway between Positions #1 and #2.)

15. Release one peg at a time along Position #2, allowing the mini-tassels to be held in place by the bullionning floss. (You will need to coax the floss to twist into bullion since the yarn bunches can hinder the twisting due to their fullness.)

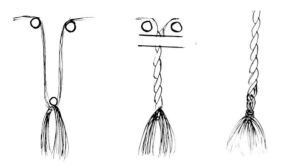

16. Once all the bullions have been formed, remove the fringe from the board, carefully removing any tape that may remain on the board.

17. Cut off the excess twisted floss above the tape and set aside.

18. Repeat the wrapping and adding of yarn bunches but for the next length of fringe, affix the tape just under the pegs on Position #1, as you would normally.

19. Make a third length of the same fringe but insert pegs along Position #3.

20. Remove the paper covering the tape on the longest (last) fringe and lay the next shorter fringe over it. Repeat for this "layer" and affix the shortest length.

21. With the shortest tassel skirt on top, affix (using glue or double-faced tape) the skirt around the lower edge of the finial.

Making the Quadruple Bullion Hanging Cord

1. Make the hanging cord using each of the floss colors cut into 1-1/2 yard lengths.

2. Knot each color of floss separately to form four separate circles. Twist and hold each color separately.

3. Put each twisted color onto one twisting tool and twist backwards to create the quadruple bullion.

4. Join the ends together to form a circle and make a large knot.

5. Insert the cord into the threading wire and thread through the center of the finial from the bottom up.

Making the Ruff

1. Measure around the lower neck of the finial, over the top edge of the skirt. Transfer this measurement to the center of the fabric.

2. Insert the fabric into the embroidery hoop with the marked measurement in the center.

3. Thread the punch needle with one strand of rose punch yarn. Refer to the illustration and punch two rows at position "B" on the needle (shorter medium length).

4. Continue punching, changing colors and loop lengths until the ruff has been completed.

5. Apply a coating of fabric glue to the flat side of the punched fabric and let dry.

6. Cut out the punched fabric close to the stitching.

7. Glue over the top of the tassel skirt with the seam in back.

Sophistication

*M*ade with a rayon/cotton subtly variegated yarn accented with a rayon overskirt, this tassel could be used either year round or for the holiday season. It could also be made in numerous color combinations. Because of the combination of techniques used to make this tassel, it's one of the more challenging projects.

Difficulty rating:
Intermediate to
Advanced Intermediate

**Finished length
(excluding bead):**
15″

Materials & Tools

- ❋ 5″ wood tassel finial with wide, flat base
- ❋ 2 yds. burgundy gimp
- ❋ 1 ball burgundy rayon crochet thread or other thin rayon cord
- ❋ 1 pkg. burgundy silk ribbon, 1/8″ wide
- ❋ 5 spools Multi's Embellishment Yarn in Woodlands color
- ❋ large-holed wooden bead, 1-1/4″ x 7/8″
- ❋ 1/2 yd. thin wire
- ❋ spray adhesive

- ❋ double-faced tape, 1/4″ wide
- ❋ cellophane tape
- ❋ twisting tool (Spinster, Corder, or pencil)
- ❋ Tassel Master with extension bed or cardboard, 9″ x 12″
- ❋ Magicord Machine or spool knitter
- ❋ crochet fork for making the ruff
- ❋ sewing machine
- ❋ sewing thread

Making the Finial

1. Spray the finial and bead with adhesive and let set.

2. For ease of twisting, you will wrap the finial with bullion cord in three sections. Cut six yards of Multi's and knot to form circle.

3. Make this into thin bullion cord by twisting it tightly, then let the yarn double back on itself to create bullion. Knot the ends to secure.

4. Repeat for two more 6-yard lengths of Multi's bullion.

5. Wrap the finial with the bullion cording, starting at the top and ending just under the "belly" of the finial. When one length ends and the next begins, apply fabric glue just before the knot, let dry, and cut off the knot. Slightly overlap the cut ends. This will make the join nearly invisible. (Try to keep the joins on what will be the back of the tassel.)

6. Wrap the burgundy gimp around the lower neck of the finial and glue to secure.

7. Bring the bullion up and around the upper neck of the finial and back down to the lower neck, wrapping it around the lower neck. Repeat for the opposite side.

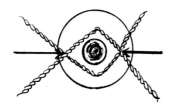

8. Glue gimp at the lower neck to secure.

9. Put a drop of fabric glue just under the gimp at the upper sides of the finial to secure.

Making the Green Underskirt

1. If you are using Tassel Master, insert a row of pegs across Position #1 on the upper bed and a row of pegs across Position #4 on the lower bed. Holding three strands of Multi's together, wrap the yarn around the pegs across the entire board. Apply tape, making sure the tape touches each strand. Remove the paper that covers the tape and remove the fringe from the board. Press together.

If you are using the cardboard, wrap the cardboard with Multi's, making sure the yarn strands do not overlap. Use all the yarn. Apply tape 1/4″ from the top of the cardboard, making sure each strand sticks to the tape. Carefully remove the fringe from the cardboard. Turn the taped side to the inside and remove the paper covering the tape. Press the front of the fringe to the back. Cut the bottom edge of the fringe.

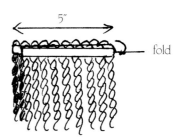

2. Fold the skirt to make a 5″ length of fringe.

3. Wrap the skirt around the lower neck of the finial, just under the "belly" and secure with wire.

Making the Burgundy Overskirt

1. Using the Magicord Machine or spool knitter, knit seven yards of burgundy crochet thread.

2. If using the Tassel Master, make the bullion fringe by inserting a row of pegs across Position #1 and Position #5 on the same board. Twist the yarn, wrap the pegs, tape across the top, and remove the lower pegs to form the bullion. Remove the fringe from the bed.

If you are using the cardboard, twist the yarn as if you were making bullion cording, as you wind the yarn around the tool. You can do this by winding the yarn in a ball spinning the ball. Wrap the frame so there will be 24 bullion fringes. Apply double-faced tape across the front and back of the fringe just below the top edge of the cardboard. Remove fringe from the cardboard. Be sure the front and back of the top of the bullion fringe sticks together.

3. Wrap the burgundy overskirt over the green underskirt and wrap a length of wire over both skirts to secure.

Making the Ruff

1. Make a 36″ length of bullion cording from one strand of burgundy crochet thread: cut a 4-1/4 yard length of crochet thread and knot the ends together to form a circle. Hang the looped end over a hook and twist. Bring the knotted end to the looped end and let the yarn double back on itself to create the bullion cording. Knot the ends to secure.

2. Position the metal bars of the crochet fork 1″ apart. Holding one strand of the burgundy bullion cording and one strand of the Multi's together, wrap the yarns around the crochet fork for 6″, taping at the edges to hold.

3. Holding a 9″ length of wire in the center of the wrapped yarn, sew a narrow zigzag stitch down the center of the frame, covering the wire as you stitch. Repeat, stitching to insure all the cording and yarn are secured.

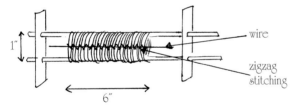

4. Remove the ruff from the frame. This is the lower ruff.

5. To create the upper ruff, repeat Steps 1 through 4, but wrap only 3″ and use a 6″ length of wire.

6. Twist the long ruff and wrap it around the base of the finial over the tassel skirts. Tie the wires at the back of tassel to secure and snip off the ends.

7. Twist the short ruff and wrap it around the top of the finial. Tie the wires to secure and snip off the ends.

Making the Wrapped Bead Accent

1. Cut one 36″ length of crochet thread and knot the ends together to form a circle. Hang the looped end over a hook and twist. Bring the knotted end to the looped end and let the yarn double back on itself to create the bullion cording. Knot the ends to secure.

2. Cover the wood bead with spray adhesive and let set.

3. Wrap the bead with the bullion thread.

Making the Wrapped Double Bullion Hanging Cord

1. Wrap the bead with burgundy gimp and secure the ends of the gimp with a drop of glue. Set aside.

2. Make a 36″ length of knitted cording using the Multi's and tie the ends to form a circle. Set aside.

3. Cut two 36″ lengths of Multi's and tie the ends to a 36″ length of the burgundy silk ribbon to form a circle.

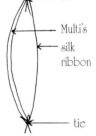

4. Twist tightly and hold.

5. Twist the knitted Multi's cording and hold.

6. Hold together the remaining burgundy bullion cording, the twisted knitted cording, and the twisted Multi's/silk ribbon, and reverse the twist to create the wrapped bullion cording.

7. Bring the ends of the cording together and knot to form a circle.

8. Insert the cord into the threading wire and draw through the base of the finial to the top.

9. Thread the bead onto the cording so it meets the top of the finial.

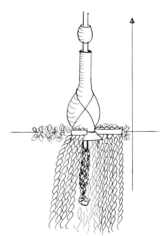

Mosaic

*W*orn beach glass bits embedded in polymer clay makes for the ideal finial top for this dramatic tassel. And the finial base? You guessed it - a deodorant cap. It has just the right surface for working and displaying the mosaic design.

Difficulty rating:
Intermediate

Finished length:
10″

Materials & Tools

- oval-shaped cap from deodorant stick
- wood wheel, 1″ diameter
- small beach glass pieces in blues/greens
- 1 package off-white Fimo
- 1 cone royal blue matte rayon yarn
- 1 spool light olive chainette yarn or rayon cord
- 1 skein olive colored cotton embroidery floss

- strong, double-sided tape
- fabric glue
- loop turner
- accordion hat rack
- fine to medium sandpaper
- drill with 1/4″ bit
- Tassel Master with extension bed

Making the Finial

1. Lightly sand the deodorant cap so the polymer clay will stick to it more readily.
2. Drill a hole in the center top of the cap.
3. Smooth the clay with your hands to cover the entire outside surface of the cap. It should be from 1/8″ to 3/16″ thick.
4. Press the glass pieces into the clay.
5. Bake at 275 degrees for 10 minutes (the plastic cap won't melt). Set aside.

Making the Blue Tassel Skirt

1. Using the Tassel Master, make three 10″ lengths of 8″ long bullion fringe with three strands of matte rayon yarn held together. Use Position #1 on the upper bed and Position #3 on the lower bed and follow the instructions that come with the Tassel Master for making bullion fringe.
2. Apply tape or stitch and remove the bullion fringe from the bed.

Making the Olive Green Tassel Overskirt

1. Fold the accordion hat rack to 9-1/2″ between pegs, measured from the center of each peg.
2. Using chainette yarn, make eight small tassels (you can make four at a time on the hat rack pegs) by making 12 wraps around the pegs.
3. Using the cotton floss, tie the wraps in the center of the pegs, tying around all the strands.
4. Stretch out the accordion rack to release the tassels. Cut the lower edge of the tassels.
5. On the Tassel Master, position one row of pegs at Position #1 and a second row at Position #2 (1-1/2″ apart).
6. Hold two strands of 2-yard lengths of chainette together and twist to create a 24″ length of bullion.

7. Fold the individual cut-edge tassels from Step 2 over the bullion.
8. Wrap the neck of each tassel three times with one strand of blue matte rayon yarn. Tie and secure with dot of glue. When the glue has dried, trim the yarn close to knot.
9. Loop the bullion and tassels around the pegs as shown, sliding up each tassel as required, and secure across the top with tape.

Making the Hanging Cord

1. Make a double bullion cord from three 2-yard lengths of matte rayon yarn and two 2-yard lengths of chainette twisted separately, joined, and reverse-twisted.
2. Join the double cord into a circle and knot.

Finishing

1. With threading wire, thread the wood wheel onto the cord until it meets the knot.
2. Remove all but the first 1/2″ of paper covering the second side of the tape on the bullion fringe.
3. Wrap around the center of the threading wire, tape side in, starting with the papered end of the tape. Repeat with the remaining three lengths of bullion fringe, but do not leave the paper on the ends.
4. Attach the small tassels and bullion cord to the inside edge of the finial, taping to the inside of cap.
5. Insert the threader into the bottom of the finial and draw it through the hole in the top, taking care not to pull in either the tassel skirt or the bullion fringe.

Flora Fancy

*M*ade from a "finial" of a foam bouquet base and silk flowers, this tassel is the perfect accent for cheering up any room. Use asters and bittersweet for a fall tassel and tulips and baby's breath for a spring accent. This tassel is so much fun to make!

Difficulty rating:
Beginner

**Finished length
(excluding hanging cord):**
12″

Materials & Tools

- 1 floral foam nosegay form
- various silk flowers and leaves, 1″ to 2″ diameter
- 1 ball burgundy rayon crochet thread or chainette
- 1 cone yellow matte rayon yarn
- glue gun
- wire cutter
- twisting tool (Spinster, Corder, or pencil)
- accordion hat rack
- Tassel Master with extension bed or Tatool with extension bed

Making the Hanging Cord

Note: This tassel is made backwards, with the hanging cord first, followed by the skirt, then the finial.

1. Cut eight 36″ strands of crochet thread or chainette. Hold them together and knot the ends to form a circle.

2. Hang the looped end over a hook and using the twisting tool of your choice, twist the yarn tightly. Bring the knotted end to the looped end and let the yarn double back on itself to create the bullion cording. Knot the ends to secure and set aside.

Making the Floral Finial

1. With wire cutters, cut off the plastic nosegay handle.

2. Make a depression in the center top of the foam with the end of a pen or pencil and hot glue the hanging cord to the foam.

3. Cut all the flower stems to 1/2″ and insert them into the foam. Glue to secure. (You won't apply the leaves until after you've attached the two tassel skirts.)

Making the Yellow Tassel Underskirt

Note: This skirt is actually eight sections, made four at a time using the accordion hat rack, and glued into the base of the floral finial.

1. Expand the hat rack so the pegs measure 9-1/2″ apart, measured from the center of the peg.

2. Wind yellow yarn around the pegs so there are a total of 16 wraps.

3. Securely tie each group of 16 wraps at one side of the peg only, then collapse the rack to release the tassels.

4. Repeat for the remaining four tassels.

5. With the end of a pen or pencil, make eight depressions in the under section of the floral finial and hot glue in the tassel skirts.

6. Trim the skirt, cutting the loops.

Making the Burgundy Overskirt

1. Make a 9″ length of 7″ long bullion fringe (Position #1 on upper board and Position #4 on lower board) with burgundy crochet thread or chainette following the instructions for making bullion fringe that come in your Tassel Master.

2. Apply double-faced tape just under the upper row of pegs.

3. Remove the paper that covers the tape and apply the skirt around the base of the floral finial, above the lip.

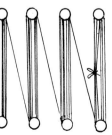

Luxe

*eant to com-
plement a luxurious and rich
decorating look, this tassel is
made more dramatic with
the addition of a filigree
finial accent embellished
with beads and a center accent mini-tassel. Note the
splayed look of this small
tassel. This is accomplished
by pressing shiny rayon,
which automatically creates
a skirt of this type.*

Difficulty rating:
Intermediate to
Advanced Intermediate

Finished length:
8˝

Materials & Tools

- 3˝ wood finial with recessed base
- wood wheel, 1˝ diameter
- 1 cone matte rayon yarn in camel color
- 1 ball matching rayon crochet thread or cord (or 3 skeins rayon embroidery floss)
- 1 yd. thin gold braid the thickness of crochet thread
- 1 yd. round gold braid, 1/8˝ diameter
- 64 gold metallic delica beads
- 19 3mm antique gold metallic faceted Czech beads
- gold eye pin jewelry finding, 1˝ long
- gold triangular filigree charm, 2˝ wide
- 26 gauge gold wire
- large-holed wood melon-shaped bead
- antique gold acrylic paint
- paintbrush
- fabric glue
- spray adhesive
- wire cutters
- strong double-sided tape
- cardboard, 1-1/2˝ x 3˝
- loop turner
- twisting tool (Spinster, Corder, or pencil)
- Tassel Master with extension bed or Tatool with extension

Making the Finial

1. Paint the wooden finial with gold paint and let dry.

2. Cut a 6″ length of wire and thread it with a sequence of 3 delica beads and 1 Czech bead until you have threaded a total of 20 beads.

3. Wind the beaded wire around the top neck of the finial and secure by twisting the wire together on the back. Trim the ends.

4. Repeat Steps 2 and 3 two times, but wrap these beaded wires around the middle neck of the finial.

5. Cut two 12″ lengths of wire and wrap them around the finial. Wrap the ends around the lower edge of the finial. Twist to secure and snip off the excess.

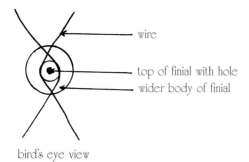

bird's eye view

wire

top of finial with hole

wider body of finial

6. Bend the filigree charm to fit around the lower edge of the finial.

7. Make one mini-tassel 1-1/4″ long from the rayon crochet thread by winding it 36 times around the 1-1/2″ width of cardboard.

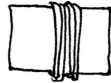

8. Insert the eye pin through the head of the mini-tassel and bend it to the top, then join just below the eye of the pin.

9. Wind a length of thin wire tightly around the neck of the mini-tassel five times.

10. Thread a 3″ piece of wire with 11 delica beads and 1 Czech bead and wrap it around the neck of the mini-tassel. Secure by twisting the wire together on the back. Snip off excess wire.

11. Thread a 6″ length of matte rayon with 11 beads in the same sequence as Step 2.

12. Tie one end of the beaded matte rayon to the lower point of the filigree charm and the other end to the eye on the top of the mini-tassel. Secure the knots with a drop of glue and snip off the excess yarn.

13. Cut a 36″ length of matte rayon. Knot the ends to form a circle and hang the looped end over a hook and twist, using the twisting tool of choice. Bring the knotted end to the looped end and let the yarn double back on itself to create the bullion cording. Knot the ends to secure.

14. Thread this small bullion cord through each end of the filigree charm, tie loosely, and set aside.

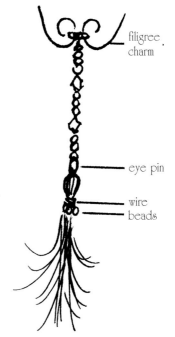

filigree charm

eye pin

wire

beads

Making the Tassel Skirt

1. Use the Tassel Master to make 6″ of 8″ long cut skirt fringe using two strands of matte rayon and one strand of shiny rayon, following the instructions for making cut skirt fringe that come with Tassel Master. Affix the tape 1/8″ lower than the directions indicate.

2. Repeat Step 1, but make bullion fringe, not cut skirt fringe, following the instructions that come with Tassel Master.

3. Remove the paper covering on the tape bullion fringe and stick the two skirts together.

4. Remove the paper on the tape from the cut skirt fringe and apply both skirts to the outer edge of the finial, with the tape facing to the inside.

5. Wrap a length of wire around the lower edge of the finial over the top edge of the skirt and cut it off. There will be excess "trim" of yarn protruding above the  skirt and wire. This serves as the narrow ruff of the tassel. Trim off the tops of the skirts to create a ruff around the finial.

6. Slip the gold filigree charm over the top of the finial to the front of the tassel and tie the cords tightly at the back, letting the cord ends hang down.

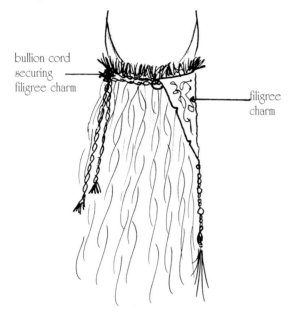

bullion cord securing filigree charm

filigree charm

Inserting the Hanging Cord & Bead

1. Apply a heavy coat of spray adhesive to the bead and let set.

2. Make a triple bullion cord from: two 2-yard lengths of matte rayon yarn for one cord component, three 2-yard lengths of shiny rayon for the second cord component, and a 1-yard length of the 1/8″ metallic braid for the third cord component. Knot the ends of each cord component separately to form three circles. Hang the matte rayon looped end over a hook and twist, using the twisting tool of choice. Tape or hold the twisted yarn. Repeat for the shiny rayon cord components. Do not twist the metallic braid. Put the two twisted components and the untwisted braid together and reverse twist to create triple bullion cord. Knot the ends to secure.

3. Make a 12″ length of cording from a 36″ length of matte rayon. Knot the ends to form a circle. Hang the looped end over a hook and twist, using the twisting tool of choice. Bring the knotted end to the looped end and let the yarn double back on itself to create the bullion cording. Knot ends to secure.

4. Holding the double bullion cord and the thin braid together, wind the yarns around the bead and secure at the ends with fabric glue.

5. Thread the cording through the large bead.

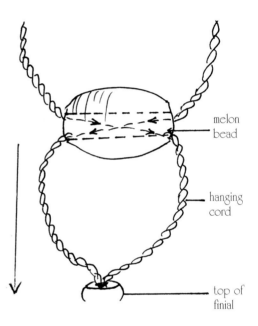

melon bead

hanging cord

top of finial

6. Thread the ends of the triple bullion cord through the top of the tassel so it comes out the bottom. Join the ends together with a large knot.

Ribbonesque

This dramatic tassel can be made in any color combination to coordinate with your decorating scheme. The ribbons give added flounce to the tassel and complement the somewhat large finial. The underskirt gives the tassel its depth and balances with the finial.

Difficulty rating:
Intermediate to
Advanced Intermediate

Finished length:
11″

Materials & Tools

- ✿ 4″ high wood newel post finial with recessed base
- ✿ wood wheel, 1-1/2″ diameter
- ✿ 10 yds. purple gimp
- ✿ 10 yds. olive gimp
- ✿ 1 ball purple Lustersheen acrylic crochet yarn (for bullion underskirt)
- ✿ 1 spool dark purple ribbon, 1/8″ wide
- ✿ 1 spool medium purple ribbon, 1/4″ wide
- ✿ 1 spool olive ribbon, 1/4″ wide

- ✿ 1 skein each gold, dark purple, light purple, dark green, and light green cotton embroidery floss
- ✿ spray adhesive
- ✿ fabric glue
- ✿ double-sided tape, 1/4″ wide
- ✿ drill press with 1/4″ bit
- ✿ vice
- ✿ cardboard, 8″ x 14″
- ✿ hairbrush

Making the Finial

1. Holding the finial upright in a vice, drill a hole through the center.
2. Spray the finial with adhesive and let set.
3. Starting at the top of the finial, wrap it with purple gimp.
4. Cut a 6-yard length of olive gimp. Knot the ends together and loop the untied end onto a hook. Twist the gimp tightly to create bullion.
5. Tie the olive bullion gimp around the lower neck of the finial and secure with a drop of fabric glue. Bring it up and around the upper neck of the finial and back down to the lower neck, wrapping it around the lower neck. Repeat on the opposite side. Secure at the lower neck with a dot of fabric glue.
6. With a 5-yard length of the dark purple ribbon, repeat the winding around the finial and secure around the lower neck with a dot of fabric glue.

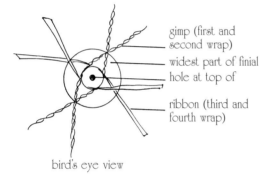

gimp (first and second wrap)

widest part of finial

hole at top of

ribbon (third and fourth wrap)

bird's eye view

Making the Tassel Skirts

1. Use the Tassel Master to make the underskirt. Insert a row of pegs in Position #1 on the upper board and another row of pegs in Position #3 on the lower board. Holding two strands of the purple crochet yarn together, make an 8″ long bullion tassel skirt across the full width of the Tassel Master board, following the directions that come with the tool.

If you are using the cardboard, wind the twisted yarn around the cardboard 20 times, tape it across the top on both the front and back just below the top of the cardboard and carefully remove the bullion fringe from the cardboard.

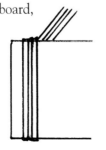

2. To make the overskirt, hold the ends of all three ribbons together and wrap them around the cardboard. Make sure the ribbons don't overlap. Make 12″ of 8″ long skirt.
3. Affix double-faced tape on the ribbon along the long end of the cardboard 1/4″ from the top edge.
4. Slide the ribbon off the cardboard and set aside.

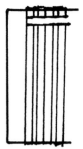

Making the Double Bullion Hanging Cord

1. To make the first cord, cut one 12-foot length each of olive gimp and purple acrylic crochet yarn. Hold both strands together and knot the ends to form a circle. Hang the looped end on a hook and twist tightly. Hold the twist using a piece of tape or a weight.
2. To make the second cord, cut one 12-foot length each of olive gimp and purple gimp. Hold both strands together and knot the ends to form a circle. Hang the looped end on the same hook and twist tightly.
3. Insert the first twisted group of yarns into the twisting tool and reverse twist all the strands. Remove from the tool. Knot the ends together to form a circle.
4. Using the stem wire folded in half for a threading wire, thread with the cording at the unknotted end.
5. Slide on the wood wheel, secured by the knot at the end of the hanging cord.

Assembling the Tassel

1. Remove all the paper from the tape on the bullion underskirt except for 1″.
2. Starting with the paper end, roll the bullion underskirt around the threading wire and secure with tape or wire.
3. Insert the stem wire with the hanging cord and wood wheel into the base of the finial.

4. Making sure the skirt is not caught up in the threading process, pull the stem wire and the hanging cord through the center of the finial so the wood wheel and the top of the skirt are pushed up against the lower end of the finial.

5. Remove the paper from the tape on the ribbon overskirt and wrap the overskirt around the edge of the base of the finial. There should be a double thickness. The ribbon will fold up and over the edge, creating its own flounce.

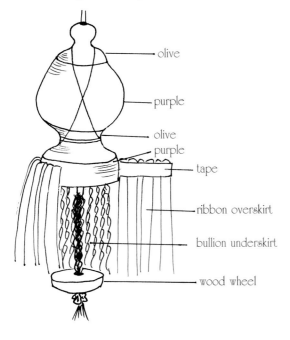

6. Cut a 120″ length of olive gimp. Tie the ends together to form a circle. Hang the loop end over a hook and twist tightly. Bring the knotted end to the loop end on the hook, letting the gimp double back on itself to form the bullion. Remove from the hook and tie the end to secure.

7. To make the five 1-1/2″ long mini-tassels, cut a 13″ length of each of the colors of floss. Holding the five strands together and brush the floss so the strands blend together. Cut into five equal lengths (approximately 2-1/2″).

8. Fold each 2-1/2″ section equally spaced over the bullion gimp and tie each of the tassel necks with a different color of floss. Trim the mini-tassels to 1-1/2″ long.

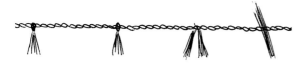

9. Fold the gimp into four equal sections and glue it equally spaced around the lower neck of the finial, above the ribbon skirt, using the photo as a guide.

Pompom Key Tassel

This type of small, fluffy tassel has been used throughout history to attach to the end of an old-fashioned key that was inserted into a chest of drawers, a trunk, or a door. Though primarily decorative, it also probably served to keep the key from being lost. This one is lots of fun to make and utilizes one of today's most common craft material: plastic canvas. The even grids of the canvas ensure the even distribution of the pompons around the neck of the tassel.

Difficulty rating:
Beginner to Intermediate

**Finished length
(excluding hanging cord):**
4˝

Materials & Tools

❦ 2-1/4˝ high wood finial with 1/4˝ hole at the top and no large hole at the bottom

❦ 3 100-yd. spools of punch embroidery yarn in pink, purple, and teal (one of each color) or very thin acrylic knitting machine yarn or 2 skeins of each color of wool Persion yarn

❦ 1 skein of each color (pink, purple, teal) cotton embroidery floss

❦ purple gimp for wrapping finial (or perle #5 cotton)

❦ 20 gauge white wrapped stem wire

❦ 1˝ wide strip of 10-mesh-to-the-inch plastic canvas to fit around the base of the finial

❦ fabric glue

❦ spray adhesive

❦ teal permanent marker

❦ round-nosed jewelry pliers

❦ threading wire

❦ twisting tool (Spinster, Corder, or pencil)

❦ umbrella swift

Making the Finial

1. Apply a thick coat of spray adhesive to the finial and let set.

2. Wrap the finial with one strand of gimp (or perle #5).

3. Use the marker to color the full length of the stem wire and let dry.

4. With round-nosed pliers, bend the wire in the shape of a flower, leaving one long end to wrap around the top of the finial.

5. Wrap the long end around the top neck of the finial and secure to the center of the wire flower.

Making the Tassel Skirt

1. Make 12 1″ pompons in each color by opening the swift to 12″ diameter and winding the punch yarn onto the swift, one color at a time. With a 12″ length of matching cotton floss, tie tightly in 12 equal sections around the swift. Remove the yarn from the swift. If you are using a jig, wind the yarn so there is a 36″ total length of yarn lengths.

2. Cut the 12 pompons evenly spaced between the tied section.

3. Fluff up the pompons by shaking them or putting them in a net bag and washing them in your clothes washer. Then, holding close to the knot, trim the bunches of yarn into a ball.

4. Measure the circumference of the lower edge of the finial and add 3/8″. Cut a strip of plastic canvas that long and three meshes wide.

5. Use the floss attached to them to tie the 36 pompons along the length of the plastic canvas, evenly distributing the three colors. The lower row should have a 1″ length of floss separating it from the canvas, the center row a 1/2″ length, and the top row should be tied closely to the canvas. (A third arm tool is very helpful for holding the plastic canvas while you tie on the pompons.)

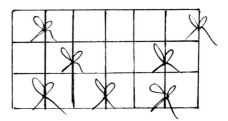

X = pompons tied and knotted on the reverse side of the plastic canvas

6. Wrap the strip of plastic canvas around the lower edge of the finial and sew the ends together with one length of floss. (Be sure not to pull the plastic canvas too tightly or you can break the plastic grids.)

Making the Triple Bullion Hanging Cord

1. Make the hanging cord by cutting one yard each of the three floss colors. Tie each length of floss into a circle. Twist each one separately, holding the twist of each one before twisting the next. Then put each of the twisted floss lengths together into the twisting tool and reverse twist to create triple bullion.

2. Knot the ends together to create a circle. Insert the hanging cord into the threading wire and pull it through the finial.

Brasilia

The fruit embell-ishment around the "cap" of the tassel and the Ama-zon-inspired color combi-nation reminded me of Brazil. The creation of the ruff is particularly easy but has a wonderful, fanciful effect. I used beads from a flea-market bracelet, so don't be too hasty when discarding your old jewelry!

Difficulty rating:
Beginner

Finished length (excluding hanging cord):
6″

Materials & Tools

❧ wood finial that comes with Tassel Master or 2-3/4″ high finial with bored-out base and lower lip

❧ 1 ball fancy sport-weight multi-colored rayon blend yarn

❧ 8 fancy beads

❧ 1 ball acrylic crochet thread or cotton embroidery floss in a color that matches the beads (I used green)

❧ 1 ball acrylic crochet thread or cotton embroidery floss in a color that contrasts with the beads (I used purple)

❧ 12″ thin wire

❧ double-faced tape, 1/4″ wide

❧ threading wire

❧ wood wheel, 1″ wide

❧ dowel, 3/8″ diameter

❧ dowel, 3/4″ diameter

❧ spray adhesive

❧ fabric glue

❧ twisting tool (Spinster, Corder, or pencil)

❧ Tassel Master or Tatool

Making the Finial

1. Apply a thick coat of spray adhesive to the finial and let set.

2. Wrap the finial with multi-colored yarn, starting at the top.

3. Thread the beads on a length of matching cotton floss and tie it to the top neck of the finial. Add a dot of glue on the knot and snip off the excess floss.

4. Evenly distribute the beads on the floss around the top of the finial.

Making the Ruff

1. Measure around the lower neck of the finial (ruff edge) and transfer this measurement to the 3/4″ diameter dowel and mark. Repeat on the 3/8″ dowel.

2. Wrap the marked length on the 3/4″ dowel with the matching crochet thread. Secure the thread ends with cello tape.

3. Wrap the marked length on the 3/8″ dowel with the contrasting crochet thread and apply cello tape on the thread ends.

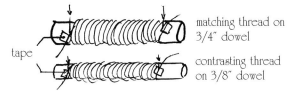

matching thread on 3/4″ dowel

tape

contrasting thread on 3/8″ dowel

4. Apply double-faced tape along the length of the crochet thread on the first dowel. Press the tape firmly to the thread, making sure all strands adhere to the tape.

5. Remove the paper covering the second side of the tape and press the 12″ wire to the center of the tape.

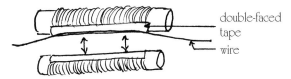

double-faced tape

wire

6. Match the second dowel to the first so the markings match and press the edge of the crochet thread to the tape.

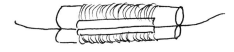

7. Remove the tape that secures the ends of the crochet yarn to the dowel. Slowly slide out the dowels.

8. Twist the ruff so the colors mix (see photo) and wrap it around the lower edge of the finial.

9. Tie the wire ends together in the back of the tassel and cut off the excess.

Making the Tassel Skirt

1. On the Tassel Master, place a row of pegs along Position #1 and a second row along Position #5 or set the Tatool to 5″.

2. Holding two strands of multi-colored yarn together, make a 10″ length of bullion fringe (across the full Tassel Master board or two lengths of the Tatool, following the instructions that come with either tool).

3. Tape or stitch across the top and remove from the board or Tatool to release the bullion fringe.

Assembling the Parts

1. Make the hanging cord with 2 yards of the multi-colored yarn and 2 yards of the matching crochet thread held together and knotted to form a circle. Hang the looped end over a hook and twist, using the twisting tool of choice. Bring the knotted end to the looped end and let the yarn double back on itself to create the bullion cording.

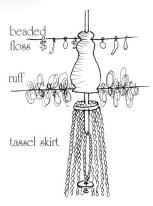

beaded floss

ruff

tassel skirt

2. Tie the ends of the bullion cord together to form a circle and knot.

3. Insert the cord into a threading wire and thread it on the wheel, sliding the wheel to the knot at the end.

4. Remove the paper from the tape on all but the first 1″ of the paper.

5. Starting at the paper-covered end, wrap the tassel skirt around the threading wire and insert it into the bottom of the finial. Draw the hanging cord through, pulling the skirt into the bottom of the finial, taking care not to catch it in the bullion skirt.

Bridal

*I*nstead of decorating the pews of the church with traditional flowers, why not add the luxe of tassels? They could also serve as memorable gifts for the wedding party and make your wedding truly unique. They are easy to make and fun as well!

Difficulty rating:
Intermediate to
Advanced Intermediate

Finished length:
9″

Materials & Tools

✤ 3″ wood finial with 3/4″ diameter hole
✤ 8 skeins cream rayon embroidery floss
✤ 8 skeins cream cotton embroidery floss
✤ 1 yd. cream satin ribbon, 1/8″ wide
✤ 1/4 yd. mini-pearls cream beaded braid, 1/2″ wide
✤ 1 faceted large-holed crystal bead, 3/4″ diameter
✤ cream-colored acrylic paint
✤ satin or matte acrylic glaze

✤ paintbrush
✤ 12″ thin wire
✤ 12″ square of weavers cloth or similar cream-colored fabric for punch embroidery
✤ fabric glue
✤ punch embroidery needle
✤ 8″ embroidery hoop
✤ twisting tool (Spinster, Corder, or pencil)
✤ Magicord Machine
✤ Tassel Master with extension bed

Making the Finial

1. Paint the finial with cream acrylic and let dry.
2. Apply the glaze and let dry.
3. Glue the faceted bead in the top of the finial opening, making sure the hole in the bead is lined up vertically. Let dry.
4. Cut two lengths of braid the circumference of the top of the finial and wrap them around the top of the finial and glue in place.

Making the Tassel Skirt

1. Separate seven skeins of rayon floss into 3-strands and tie end-to-end to create one long length. (Due to rayon's tendency to not hold a knot, place a dab of fabric glue on the knots.)
2. Repeat with the cotton floss.
3. Thread the Magicord Machine with one 3-strand end of each of the rayon and cotton held together.
4. Knit all the floss into cording.
5. On the Tassel Master, place a row of pegs along Position #1 on the upper bed and a row of pegs along Position #2 on the lower bed.
6. Make 12″ of 7″ long bullion fringe from the knitted cording. (Don't twist the cording tightly.)
7. Apply double-faced tape along the top and remove the tassel skirt from the board.
8. Remove the paper from the second side of the tape and wrap the tassel skirt around the base (ruff edge) of the finial.
9. Wrap the 12″ wire over the top of the skirt and tighten. Snip off the excess wire.

Making the Ruff

1. Measure around the lower neck of the finial over the top edge of the skirt. Transfer this measurement to the center of the fabric.
2. Separate one skein of rayon and cotton floss into 3-strand lengths.
3. Thread the punch needle with one 3-strand length of rayon and one 3-strand length of cotton. Adjust the punch needle to create 1/4″ long loops, following the manufacturer's instructions.
4. Punch four rows of the floss between the marks on the fabric.

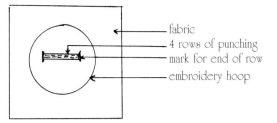

fabric
4 rows of punching
mark for end of row
embroidery hoop

5. Apply a coating of fabric glue on the wrong side of the fabric to secure the loops. Let dry.
6. Cut out the punched section close to the stitching.

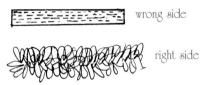

wrong side

right side

7. Apply a 1/2″ wide strip of glue over the wire covering the top of the tassel skirt.
8. Wrap the punched fabric around the lower neck of the finial over the top of the skirt. Glue the ends to secure.

Making the Single Bullion Hanging Cord

1. Cut two 36″ lengths each of cotton floss and rayon floss.
2. Cut one 36″ length of 1/8″ wide ribbon.
3. Tie the ribbon and combined flosses securely at each end to form a circle.
4. Hang over a hook and twist.
5. Join the ends together and let the yarn double back on itself to create bullion cord.
6. Fold in half, knot at one end, and draw the cord through the tassel. The bead at the top of the finial will hold the knot in place.

China

Tassels have been used for many centuries in China, so I feel no tassel-making book is complete without at least one design honoring that ancient tradition. Colors most commonly used seem to be red, of course, and shades of green (jade) and gold or brass.

Difficulty rating:
Beginner to Intermediate

**Finished length
(excluding hanging cord):**
11″

Materials & Tools

❦ 2 cut jade beads, 1-3/4″ diameter
❦ 1 filigree bead cap, 3/4″ diameter
❦ 3 gold beads, 2mm
❦ 2 antique gold filigree beads, 3/8″ diameter
❦ end pin, 4″ long
❦ gold jump ring, 4mm
❦ 1 ball red rayon crochet thread
❦ 3 yds. gold rayon crochet thread or 1 skein rayon embroidery floss

❦ cardboard tube, 3/8″ diameter x 3/4″ long
❦ red paint
❦ fabric glue
❦ dental floss threader
❦ twisting tool (Spinster, Corder, or pencil)
❦ Tassel Master with extension or cardboard, 8-1/2″ x 11″

Making the Tassel Skirt

1. Paint the cardboard tube and let dry.

2. If using the Tassel Master, insert one row of pegs along Position #1 on the upper board and another row of pegs on Position #3 on the lower board.

3. Wind a double strand of red rayon thread around the Tassel Master board or the piece of cardboard, keeping the strands on the cardboard just touching each other but not overlapping for 5".

4. Apply double-faced tape below the pegs of the Tassel Master or 1/8" below the top of the cardboard. Carefully remove the thread from the board or cardboard. Press all threads to the tape to ensure that each one sticks.

5. Remove the protective paper from the tape. With the tape side in and the upper edge of the tape matching the top edge of the tube, wrap the fringe around the painted tube.

6. Cut the lower edge of the tassel.

7. Insert the end pin through the underside of the bead cap.

8. Attach the bead cap to the top of the tassel by squeezing the edges around the top of the tassel skirt and tube.

Making the Finial

1. Thread the end pin bottom to top with a filigree bead, jade bead, 2mm bead, filigree bead, 2mm bead, jade bead, 2mm bead.

2. Bend the top of the head pin into a loop for the hanging cord.

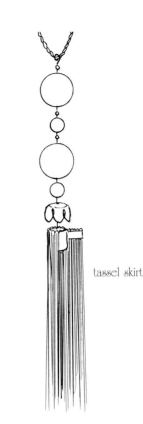

tassel skirt

Making the Double Bullion Hanging Cord

1. Make the first cord using two 36" lengths of the gold thread held together with the ends knotted to form a circle. Hang the looped end over a hook and twist tightly. Hold the twisted cord with tape or a weight while you twist the second cord.

2. Make the second cord like the first but use one 36" length of gold and one 36" length of red thread held together. Do not remove from the twisting tool.

3. Insert the first twisted thread group into the twisting tool and reverse twist to create the double bullion cord. Knot the ends to create a circle, then double the cord.

4. With jewelry pliers, open the loop at the top of the end pin slightly and insert the hanging cord.

5. Knot the cord together at the top to form a circle. Snip the ends to even off.

Della Robbia Holiday Tassel

*T*he perfect accent for any holiday décor, this tassel is easy and inexpensive to make but definitely makes quite a statement. The finial is just three ordinary wood pieces (a ball drawer knob, a flat drawer knob, and a candle cup) joined together and accented with a tapered candle ornament "ruff." Couldn't be much simpler!

Difficulty rating:
Beginner to Intermediate

Finished length
(excluding hanging cord):
10″

Materials & Tools

* round drawer knob with flat base, 1-1/4″ diameter
* wood candle cup, 1-1/4″ diameter
* flat top drawer pull, 1-1/2″ diameter
* wood wheel, 1″ diameter
* acrylic paint in dark green and burgundy
* matte finish glaze
* paintbrush
* embroidery floss: 2 skeins pale gold, 2 skeins dark green, 4 skeins burgundy
* 10 yds. each chainette yarn: pale gold, willow green
* 1 spool cranberry chainette yarn
* 1 della-robbia type tapered candle ornament (the kind that circles the base of a standard tapered candle)
* tacky glue
* fabric glue
* tape
* threading wire
* hand or electric drill with 1/4″ bit
* cardboard, 3-1/2″ wide x any length
* twisting tool (Spinster, Corder, or pencil)
* Tassel Master or sturdy cardboard, 11″ x 12

Making the Finial

1. Drill a 1/4˝ hole in the center of the candle cup, flat drawer pull, and the round drawer knob.

2. Paint each wood component separately. Paint the round knob and the candle cup green and the flat top drawer pull burgundy.

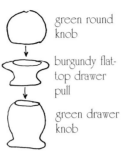

green round knob

burgundy flat-top drawer pull

green drawer knob

3. Use tacky glue to glue the components together as shown. Let dry.

4. Apply matte glaze and let dry.

5. Wrap a strand of gold chainette around each finial component where they join and glue in place, using the photo as a guide.

6. Wrap dark green embroidery floss three times around the center of the flat-top drawer pull and glue in place.

Making the Tassel Skirt

1. If you are using the Tassel Master, insert a row of pegs along Position #1 and a second row along Position #5. With one strand of cranberry chainette and one strand of burgundy embroidery floss together, twist the yarns and make 10˝ of bullion fringe (the full width of the Tassel Master board). Tape or stitch the top of the bullion and release the pegs or remove the yarn from the frame to create bullion. Set aside.

If you are using the cardboard, wind the two twisted yarns around the cardboard 20 times, tape it across the top on both the front and back just below the top of the cardboard, and carefully remove the bullion fringe from the cardboard.

2. Make six mini-tassels, two of each color group: pale gold chainette and gold color floss; willow green chainette and dark green floss; cranberry chainette and burgundy floss. Wrap the 3-1/2˝ wide cardboard ten times with two strands of embroidery floss and one strand of chainette held together for each color group. Tie in the *center* just to secure the group of yarn (you will be removing this tie later) and remove from the cardboard. Cut each tassel along the lower edge and attach, fringe-style (see illustration), to the undersection of the candle ornament, evenly spacing and alternating the colors.

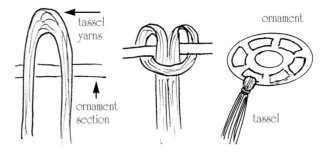

tassel yarns

ornament section

ornament

tassel

3. Put a drop of fabric glue on the upper back of the tassels. Set aside.

Making the Double Bullion Hanging Cord

1. Make a hanging cord using two cords held together. Make the first cord using two 36˝ lengths of willow green chainette held together with the ends knotted to form a circle. Hang the looped end over a hook and twist tightly. Hold the twisted cord with tape or a weight while you twist the second cord.

2. Make the second cord as the first but use two 36˝ strands of cranberry chainette held together. Do not remove from the twisting tool.

3. Insert the first twisted cord into the twisting tool and reverse twist to create the double bullion cord. Knot the ends to create a circle, then double the cord.

Assembling the Tassel

1. Insert a threading wire through the cord and slide it down the wheel to the knot.

2. Wrap the skirt around the threading wire, tape side in for Tassel Master users or wrap the tape around the top of the skirt.

3. Insert the ends of the threading wire through the wide opening in the candle cup and pull it through, making sure the skirt doesn't get caught.

4. Ease the skirt into the base of the candle cup and finish pulling through the cording.

5. Slide the candlestick ornament with the mini-tassels attached over the hanging cord and the finial so it sits on the lip edge of the cup. Bend the "fruits" and leaves over to hide the lower edges of the candle ornament.

Large Cowrie Shell Tassel

After looking at the hollow bottoms of shells, it came to mind that these gifts of nature would make wonderful finials. Small shell tassels are perfect in a bathroom and larger ones would work well in a seaside home. You could also use them as curtain finials with matching tassel accents. Try using a different type of shell for each tassel in your decorating plan.

Difficulty rating:
Beginner

Finished length (excluding hanging cord):
8″

Materials & Tools

- 1 large cowrie shell
- 15 small shells of various types
- few yds. light taupe rayon bouclé yarn
- few yds. white cotton string
- few yds. brown tweed yarn

- double-faced tape, 1/4″ wide
- glue gun
- twisting tool (Spinster, Corder, or pencil)
- Tassel Master or cardboard, 8″ x 7″ and 5″ x 7″

Making the Finial

1. Actually, some sea creature has already made the finial for you. Just make sure there are openings on both ends to insert a hanging cord.

Making the Tassel Skirts

1. Measure the long opening on the cowrie shell.

2. To make the *front skirt* on the Tassel Master, insert a row of pegs across Position #1 and Position #5 or use the 5″ x 7″ piece of cardboard.

3. Holding one strand of bouclé and one strand of string together, make a cut-edge fringe the width of the opening of the cowrie shell, following instructions that come with the tool. If you are using cardboard, wind the yarns around the cardboard to equal the width of the opening in the shell.

4. Apply a row of double-faced tape across the top according the instructions that come with Tassel Master or along the top on both the front and back of the fringe on the cardboard. Remove the yarn from the tool or cardboard. Cut the fringe along the lower edge. Set aside.

5. To make the *rear skirt* on the Tassel Master, insert a row of pegs across Position #1 on the upper board and across Position #2 of the lower board or use the 8″ x 7″ piece of cardboard.

6. Repeat the wrapping as above, but with just one strand of the brown tweed. Affix the double-faced tape across the top as above.

7. Remove the skirt from the tool or cardboard. Cut the lower edge of the fringe.

8. Remove the paper from the double-faced tape from the front skirt and apply it to the back skirt.

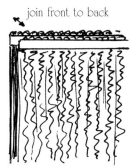

join front to back

9. Remove the paper from the tape of the back skirt and apply both skirts to the opening of the cowrie shell with the tape of the back skirt securing both skirts to the shell. (Depending on the size of the opening of your shell, you may choose to affix the skirt after adding the hanging cord.)

10. Glue 5 mini shells to the string equidistant from each other but at varying heights. Snip off excess string.

Making the Single Bullion Hanging Cord

1. Make a single bullion hanging cord using two yards of the rayon bouclé yarn and two yards of the string held together. Knot the ends together to form a circle. Hang the looped end over a hook and twist. Bring the knotted end to the looped end and let the yarn double back on itself to create the bullion cording. Knot the ends to secure and set aside.

2. Knot each end of the bullion cord. (Do not knot together to form circle.)

3. Insert the knots into the openings at the both ends of the shell and glue to secure.

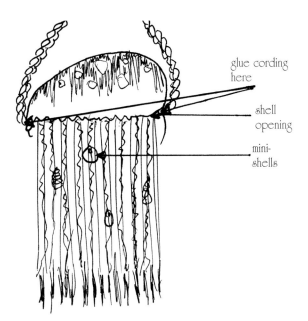

glue cording here

shell opening

mini-shells

Antique Accent

This accent tassel lends a bit of drama and a touch of elegance to a home decorating scheme. It looks particularly good hanging by itself on a large ornament hanger on a sofa table or on a bookcase. The thick but very drapey knitted cording is balanced with the somewhat large finial.

Difficulty rating:
Intermediate to
Advanced Intermediate

Finished length:
11″

Materials & Tools

❀ 4″ high wood newel post finial with recessed base (found at lumber yards)
❀ 1 small tube metallic gold acrylic paint
❀ 4 spools Antique color Multi's Embellishment Yarn (160 yards total)
❀ 1 skein toast color cotton embroidery floss
❀ 28 small antique gold barrel beads
❀ 1 large-hole antique gold barrel bead
❀ 1/2 yd. off-white braided trim, 1/4″ wide

❀ strong double-faced tape, 1/4″ wide
❀ fabric glue
❀ paintbrush
❀ stem wire
❀ drill press with 1/4″ bit
❀ twisting tool (Spinster, Corder, or pencil)
❀ dental floss threader
❀ Magicord Machine or spool knitter
❀ Tassel Master with extension board

Making the Finial - Step 1

1. Holding the finial upright in the drill press vice, drill a hole through the center.
2. Paint the finial with gold metallic and set aside to dry.

Making the Tassel Skirt

1. Using the Magicord Machine or spool knitter, knit all Multi's yarn except 10 yards.
2. Use the Tassel Master to make an 8″ long bullion tassel skirt. Place the pegs in Position #1 on the upper board and in Position #3 on the lower board. Wrap the cording from Step 1 across 1-1/2 widths of the bed (15″). Do not twist the cording tightly.
3. Break off the cording and weave the end yarn through the loops to secure. Tape across the top of the fringe and remove the bullion from the board. Set aside.

Making the Double Bullion Hanging Cord

1. To make the first cord, cut two 12-foot lengths of embroidery floss. Hold both strands together and knot the ends to form a circle. Hang the looped end on a hook and twist tightly. Hold the twist with tape or a weight until you have twisted the second cord.
2. To make the second cord, cut one 12-foot length of the antique yarn. Knot the ends to form a circle. Hang the looped end on a hook and twist tightly. Do not remove from the twisting tool.
3. Insert the first group of twisted yarns into the twisting tool and reverse twist all the strands. Knot the ends together to form a circle. Fold in half twice for a double cord and make a large knot at the end.
4. Using the stem wire folded in half, thread with the cording at the unknotted end and draw it through the finial.
5. Slide on the large-holed bead until it meets the top of the finial.

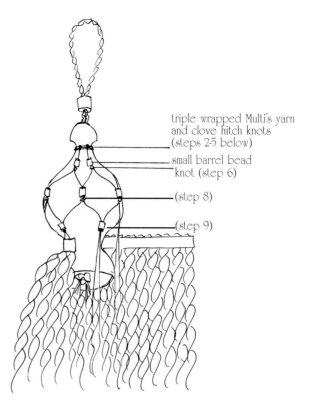

triple wrapped Multi's yarn and clove hitch knots (steps 2-5 below)
small barrel bead knot (step 6)
(step 8)
(step 9)

Making the Finial - Step 2

Tip: For ease of embellishing the finial without catching the skirt, wrap and tape a sheet of paper, plastic, or fabric around the skirt.

1. Remove the paper from the exposed side of the tape and with the tape facing toward the finial, wrap the bullion skirt around the lower neck of the finial.
2. Cut an 18″ length of Multi's yarn and triple it. Cut four 3-foot lengths of Multi's yarn.
3. Using a clove-hitch knot, attach each of the four 3-foot lengths of yarn to the tripled yarn.
4. Tie the tripled length of yarn to the upper neck

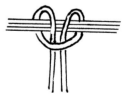

of the finial and knot to secure. Apply a dot of glue to the knot, let dry, and snip off the yarn ends.
5. Spread the knotted lengths of yarn equally around the finial neck.

6. Thread one small bead onto a double strand of yarn and tie a knot under the bead to hold it in place.

7. Repeat around three more times, using the photo as a guide.

8. Separate each group of two and put together one strand from one group and one from the adjacent group and thread with another bead. Secure with a knot (refer to the illustration).

9. Repeat Step 8.

10. Make a second set of knots as for Step 8 but do not include the bead.

11. Cut a 2-foot length of Multi's yarn and wrap it around the lower neck of the finial over the top edge of the skirt, catching in the beaded strands. Tie the knot securely.

12. Repeat Step 8 once more, this time attaching the bead and knotting securely beneath the bead.

13. Thread a bead onto each of the eight lengths of yarn and make a knot beneath the beads, 1″ below the knot above it. Put a dot of glue on each of the eight end knots. Cut off the excess yarn.

14. Wrap braided trim twice around the lower neck of the finial and secure with glue. Cut off excess braid.

15. Cut a 36″ length of Multi's yarn and knot the ends together to form a circle. Hang the looped end over a hook and twist. Bring the knotted end to the looped end and let the yarn double back on itself to create the bullion cording. Knot the ends to secure.

16. Thread the remaining four beads onto the bullion cord. Tie the cord around the lower neck of the finial, evenly spacing the beads on the cord around the neck over the trim. Tie the ends and apply a dot of glue. Let dry and cut off the ends of the cording.

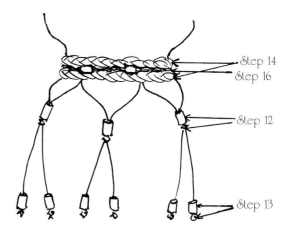

Eleganza

This tassel is an elaboration of some very basic techniques used in combination with each other. The beads are an easy but dramatic accent to an otherwise relatively basic design.

Difficulty rating:
Beginner to
Intermediate

**Finished length
(excluding hanging cord):**
7″

Materials & Tools

- ❦ wood finial that comes with Tassel Master or 2-3/4″ high finial with bored-out base and lower lip
- ❦ 2 spools Multi's Embellishment Yarn, color Berryvine
- ❦ 1 package or strand of delica beads in purple/green aurora borealis
- ❦ 1 skein dark green cotton embroidery floss
- ❦ dark teal green permanent marker
- ❦ double-faced tape, 1/4″ wide
- ❦ fabric glue
- ❦ spray adhesive
- ❦ masking tape

- ❦ threading wire
- ❦ 10″ length of thin florist's wire
- ❦ wood wheel, 1″ diameter with 1/4″ center hole
- ❦ dental floss threader or beading needle
- ❦ dowel, 12″ x 1/4″ diameter
- ❦ dowel, 12″ x 1/8″ diameter
- ❦ twisting tool (Spinster, Custom Corder, or pencil)
- ❦ Magicord Machine or spool knitter
- ❦ Tassel Master, Tatool, or sturdy cardboard, 5″ x 12″

Making the Finial

1. Wrap masking tape around the fullest (bottom) section of the finial and apply a thick coat of spray adhesive to the top two sections. Let set.

2. Remove the masking tape and color the unsprayed section with the teal marker. Let dry.

3. Starting at the top of the finial, wrap the top section with dark green floss.

4. Wrap the next section with one strand of Multi's.

5. Cut a 6˝ length of Multi's and tie it loosely around the neck just completed.

6. Cut four 20˝ lengths of Multi's and attach them to the 6˝ strand around the neck using the clove hitch.

7. Tie the 6˝ length of Multi's securely and apply a drop of glue to secure the knot.

8. Using the four 20˝ lengths of Multi's, make four square knots around the finial.

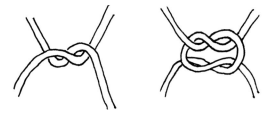

9. Repeat for the adjacent threads.

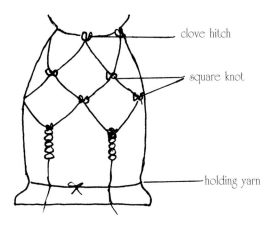

- clove hitch
- square knot
- holding yarn

10. Thread each of the four double strands of Multi's with five beads. Knot just under the beads to secure.

11. Cut a 10˝ length of Multi's and tie it around the base of the finial to pull in the knotted and beaded yarn.

12. Distribute the beaded yarn groups evenly around the lower edge and apply a dot of glue over each to secure. Snip off the excess thread.

13. Cut a 10˝ length of Multi's, thread on one bead, and knot. Repeat until there are 16 beads and knots.

14. Wrap the beaded yarn around the top neck of the finial and tie it in back to secure. Apply a dot of glue to the knot and snip off the excess yarn.

Making the Ruff

1. Thread a 60˝ length of Multi's with 72 beads.

2. Mark the center 5˝ of each dowel and wrap the 1/4˝ dowel between the marks with the beaded Multi's from Step 1, pushing up one bead on each wrap.

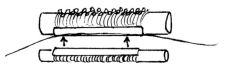

3. Apply double-faced tape along the length of the yarn opposite the beads.

4. Wrap and apply tape to the 1/8˝ dowel in the same way as the 1/4˝, omitting the beads.

5. Remove the paper from the tape on both dowels.

6. Press florist's wire to one of the lengths of tape.

7. Press the dowels together so the tapes match, enclosing the wire. Carefully remove the dowels from the wrapped yarn.

8. Twist the yarn loops to form the ruff.

Making the Tassel Skirt

1. Cut a 2-yard length of Multi's and set aside for the hanging cord.

2. Knit the remaining Multi's on the Magicord Machine or spool knitter.

3. If using the Tassel Master, place a row of pegs along Position #1 and a second row along Position #5. If using the Tatool, adjust for a 5″ long fringe.

4. Twist the cording lightly and wrap it around the pegs, Tatool, or cardboard.

5. Apply tape below the upper pegs or 1/8″ from the edge of the cardboard.

6. Carefully remove the fringe from the board or tool to create bullion, making sure the tape sticks to each strand.

Making the Single Bullion Hanging Cord

1. Fold the remaining knitted Multi's yarn into thirds.

2. Thread one of those thirds with randomly spaced beads, making sure they are separated from each other (or threading the cord through the finial will be challenging).

3. Twist the cording to create a single bullion.

4. Knot the ends together to create a circle.

Assembling the Tassel

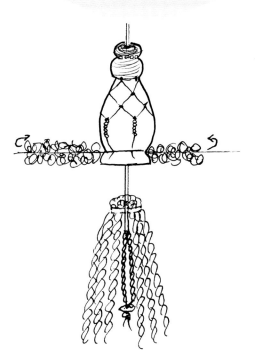

1. Insert the hanging cord into the threading wire and thread it on the wheel, sliding it to the knot at the end.

2. Remove all but the first 1/2″ of the paper from the tape on the bullion fringe.

3. Starting at the paper-covered end, wrap the skirt around the threading wire and insert the threading wire into the bottom of the finial.

4. Draw the cord through, pulling the skirt into the bottom of the finial.

5. Wrap the ruff around the lower edge of the finial, twisting the wires together to secure. Snip off the excess wire.

Project Fiesta

This fun and festive tassel incorporates both purchased and "trash to treasure" components. It's a great tassel to display for an "event" party, in a teenager's room, or for just plain fun. Alternatively, you could use the basic concept of Fiesta and change the colors for a much more understated look.

Difficulty rating:
Intermediate

Finished length:
16˝

Materials & Tools

- wood bowl, 2-3/4˝ diameter
- cardboard tube, 2-3/4˝ diameter x 2-1/2˝
- small sheet foam board, cut into a 3˝ circle with 1/4˝ diameter hole in center
- fuchsia acrylic paint
- paintbrush
- 2 balls fuchsia acrylic crochet yarn
- 1 ball purple acrylic crochet yarn
- fuchsia poly fleece, 13˝ x 15˝
- 1 yd. fancy beaded trim (available at specialty trim or fabric stores)
- rubber band
- strong tape, 1/4˝ wide
- plastic drinking straw
- spray adhesive
- drill with 1/4˝ bit
- threading wire
- twisting tool (Spinster, Corder, or pencil)
- Magicord Machine or spool knitter
- Tassel Master with extension board
- spacer board, 3˝ wide x 10˝ long x 3/4˝ thick (cut from wood or foam packing)
- dowel, 6˝ long x 1/4˝ diameter

Making the Finial

1. Paint the cardboard tube and foam board circle with fuchsia paint. Let dry.

2. Drill a hole in the center of the wood bowl.

3. Apply spray adhesive to outside of the bowl and the outside of the painted cardboard tube and let set.

4. Turn the bowl hole-side-up and place it on top of the cardboard tube and glue the edges. Let dry.

5. Glue beaded trim around the edge of the bowl, just above where it is glued to the cardboard tube.

6. Wind purple yarn around the top of the bowl (the side with the drilled hole). Switch to fuchsia yarn and continue winding around the bowl to within 1/2″ of the beaded trim. Switch back to purple and continue winding around the bowl until it meets the cardboard tube, just above the beaded trim.

7. Turn the finial upside down so the beaded trim hangs toward the bowl and, with fuchsia yarn, continue winding until the cardboard core is covered entirely.

Making the Tassel Skirt

1. Cut 1/4″ strips of fringe into the fleece along the 15″ length, leaving 1″ uncut at the top.

2. Using the Magicord Machine or manual spool knitter, knit 1-1/2 balls of fuchsia yarn, wrapping the cording around the dowel as you knit.

3. Use the Tassel Master to make 7″ of 12″ long bullion tassel skirt. Place pegs in Position #1 on the upper board and Position #5 on the lower board with the spacer board dividing them. Wind with the corded yarn from Step 2 above.

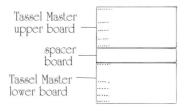

Do not twist the cording tightly.

4. Apply tape across the top of the cording and remove the yarn from the board.

5. Cut off seven of the beaded fringe sections from the beaded trim and sew them to the lower edge of seven of the bullion fringe sections, evenly spaced.

Making the Double Bullion Hanging Cord

1. To make the first cord, cut one 3-yard length of purple yarn. Triple it and knot the ends to form a circle. Hang the looped end over a hook and twist tightly. Hold the twisted cord with tape or a weight while you twist the second cord.

2. To make the second cord, repeat Step 1 with a 3-yard length of fuchsia yarn. Do not remove from the twisting tool.

3. Insert the first twisted yarn group into the twisting tool and reverse twist to create the double bullion cord. Knot the ends to create a circle.

4. Fold the hanging cord in half and make an extra-large knot.

5. Using the threading wire folded in half, thread with the cording at the unknotted end.

Assembling the Tassel

1. Slide the foam board circle on the hanging cord to the knot

2. Roll the fleece fringe (with the uncut section on top) around the drinking straw and secure with tape.

3. Roll the bullion fringe around the fleece and secure with a rubber band. Set aside.

4. Insert the threading wire through the bottom of the finial and pull through the hanging cord, pulling the skirt into the base of the finial.

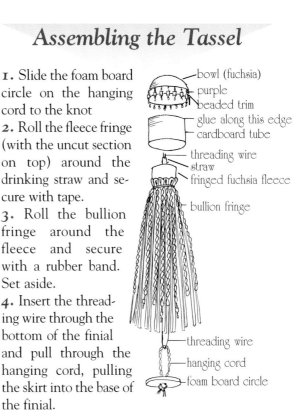

bowl (fuchsia)
purple
beaded trim
glue along this edge
cardboard tube
threading wire
straw
fringed fuchsia fleece
bullion fringe
threading wire
hanging cord
foam board circle

Circus Circus

*J*ust for fun and particularly suited to a colorful children's room, this tassel was created with the kinds of craft components you may already have from crafting with your kids: chenille stems, felt, embroidery floss, and Pom-Beadz. Its finial is an empty thread spool.

Difficulty rating:
Beginner to Intermediate

**Finished length
(excluding hanging cord):**
6″

Materials & Tools

- 1 empty thread spool (the long, thin European thread type)
- 1 skein embroidery floss in red, orange, yellow, green, and blue
- 75 Pom-Beadz in primary colors, 1/2″ diameter
- 1 each blue and red chenille stems
- 1 small piece red felt
- 2″ grosgrain ribbon, 1/4″ wide (I used red with blue edging but plain red is fine)
- spray adhesive
- fabric glue
- threading wire
- double-faced tape, 1/4″ wide
- twisting tool (Spinster, Custom Corder, or pencil)
- crochet fork
- dowel, 1/8″ diameter, or #5 or #6 knitting needle

Making the Finial

1. Apply a thick coat of spray adhesive to the spool and let set.

2. Holding all colors of embroidery floss together in rainbow sequence, wrap the spool with floss.

3. Wrap the top edge of the spool with the 2″ length of ribbon and glue in place.

4. Trace the top of the spool on the felt and cut out the shape including the center hole.

5. Glue the felt circle to the top of the spool.

Making the Tassel Skirt

1. Position the crochet fork to create a 4″ long skirt.

2. Tie each of the colors of floss to the frame in a rainbow sequence and thread each with 10 Pom-Beadz in the matching color of floss.

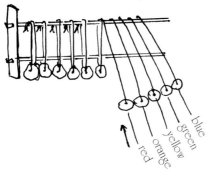

3. Wrap the frame, sliding the bead to the lower edge of each wrap. The floss at the top of the frame may be widely spaced due to the thickness of the beads.

4. Wrap so that three beads of each color have been threaded on.

5. Apply double-faced tape across the top, making sure each strand of floss adheres to the tape. Slide the floss off the crochet fork and set aside.

6. Reposition the bars of the frame so the skirt will measure 3″ long.

7. Repeat the wrapping and taping, but use four beads per color. Slide the floss off the crochet fork and set aside.

8. Reposition the bars of the frame so the skirt will measure 2″ long.

9. Repeat the wrapping and taping, but use three beads per color. Slide the floss of the crochet fork and set aside.

10. Remove the paper from the second side of the tape on all three tassel skirts and tape them together.

11. With the tape side in, carefully (to avoid tangling the beads) wrap the skirt around the base of the spool.

Making the Ruff

1. Wind each chenille stem around the dowel or knitting needle to create a "curly-q" and slide it off.

2. Wrap the red chenille stem around the base of the spool over the top edge of the skirt, stretching to fit, and hook together in the back to join.

3. Repeat for the blue stem, but position it just above the red one, over the lower center shaft of the spool.

Making the Single Bullion Hanging Cord

1. Hold two yards of each color of floss together and knot to form a circle.

2. Hang the looped end over a hook and twist tightly.

3. Join the ends, letting the yarn double back on itself to create the bullion.

4. Knot the ends together to form a circle.

Assembling the Tassel

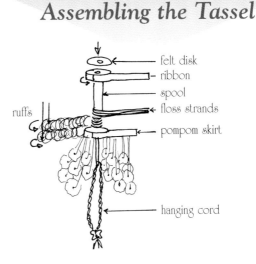

1. Thread the hanging cord into the threading wire.

2. Thread it into the bottom of the spool, taking care not to catch in any of the skirt.

Spiral

After looking at an unusual chandelier, I had the idea to create a similar look with a tassel. While there are numerous designs for chandeliers and while bullion fringe can hardly be compared to cut crystal, the look is a bit similar. So have fun with this - try spiraling a double skirt, one with beads at the bottom, and other looks.

Difficulty rating:
Beginner to Intermediate
Finished length:
10˝

Materials & Tools

- ❦ finished wood bead with large hole, 1-3/4˝ x 1-1/4˝ diameter
- ❦ 1˝ round unfinished wood bead with large hole
- ❦ 3/4˝ round finished wood bead with large hole
- ❦ 5˝ ombre ribbon in yellow tones, 1/4˝ wide
- ❦ 1 cone yellow matte rayon yarn
- ❦ 24˝ length of 2 plies of yellow cotton embroidery floss
- ❦ double-faced tape, 1/4˝ wide
- ❦ fabric glue
- ❦ threading wire
- ❦ tapestry needle
- ❦ tacky glue
- ❦ bag clip or spring clip
- ❦ twisting tool (Spinster, Custom Corder, or pencil)
- ❦ Tassel Master, Tatool, or crochet fork

Making the Finial

1. Cut a 36″ length of yarn and separate the plies.

2. Thread the yarn through the hole in the unfinished bead and tie to secure.

3. Thread the two strands of floss on the tapestry needle and tie to the yarn attached to the bead. Vertically wrap the 1″ round bead.

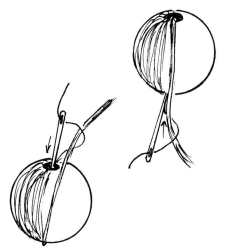

4. Cut the ribbon at an angle and glue it around the oblong bead in an X (refer to the photo).

5. Glue all three beads together, with the oblong on the bottom, the 1″ round in the center, and the 3/4″ round on top. Let dry.

Making the Single Bullion Hanging Cord

1. Hold three 1-1/2 yard lengths of yarn together and knot the ends to form a circle.

2. Hang the looped end over a hook and twist. Bring the knotted end to the looped end and let the yarn double back on itself to create the bullion cording.

3. Knot one end of the bullion cord. Apply a liberal amount of fabric glue around the cording just above the knot. Let dry and cut off the knot.

4. Thread the loop end of the cord into the threading wire, then through the finial. Leave 5″ of cord below the finial. Attach the bag clip or spring clip at the top of the finial.

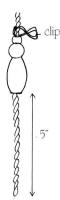
clip

.5″

Making the Tassel Skirt

1. On the Tassel Master, place a row of pegs along Position #1 and a second row along Position #3. Or set up the Tatool or crochet fork to make a 2-1/2″ long fringe.

2. Holding one strand of yarn, make a 20″ length of bullion fringe (across two full Tassel Master boards or the crochet fork, or four lengths on the Tatool) following instructions that come with the tool.

3. Apply tape along the top of the fringe and remove it from the board, fork, or Tatool.

4. Remove the paper from the second side of the tape. Beginning at the glued end of the 5″ of hanging cord protruding from the bottom of the finial, wrap the bullion fringe around the hanging cord in a spiral direction, taking care not to catch the fringe in the tape.

5. When all 5″ of the hanging cord are wrapped, cut off the fringe and glue the end just below the large bead.

6. Pull the hanging cord and the top 1/2″ of the spiral fringe into the lower bead to hide the top edge of the fringe.

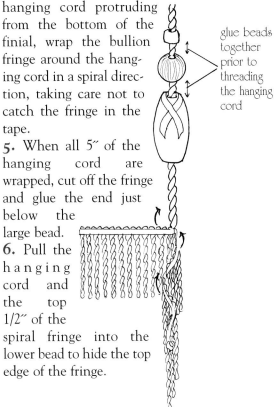

glue beads together prior to threading the hanging cord

In the Pink

*U*tilizing only the very basic instructions for making a finial-topped tassel, this is just one of the many variations you can achieve by simple yarn-wrapping, then catch-stitch netting the top of a basic finial. Then use rayon sewing thread knitted on a simple I-cord-maker for the tassel skirt and embellish with glued-on mini ribbon roses.

Difficulty rating:
Beginner to Intermediate

Finished length
(excluding hanging cord)
6-1/2″

Materials & Tools

- ☀ wood finial that comes with Tassel Master or 2-3/4″ high finial with bored-out base and lower lip
- ☀ 2 spools rose rayon sewing machine embroidery thread
- ☀ 1 skein each cream and light rose perle #5 cotton
- ☀ 1 skein dark rose perle #3 cotton
- ☀ 8 small, light pink ribbon roses

- ☀ double-faced tape, 1/4″ wide
- ☀ fabric glue
- ☀ spray adhesive
- ☀ threading wire
- ☀ wheel, 1″ diameter
- ☀ twisting tool (Spinster, Custom Corder, or pencil)
- ☀ Magicord Machine or spool knitter
- ☀ Tassel Master or Tatool

Making the Finial

1. Apply a thick coat of spray adhesive to the finial and let set.

2. Wrap the finial with one strand of each color of the perle #5 held together, starting at the top. Be sure not to twist the yarn as you wrap.

3. Cut a 2-foot length of perle #3 and tie it securely around the second neck of the finial. Apply a dot of glue on the knot.

4. Work the catch stitch around the "belly" of the finial and secure it around the lower edge with a knot. Apply a dot of glue to the knot and snip off the excess.

Making the Tassel Underskirt

1. Holding both strands of the rayon thread together, thread the Magicord or spool knitter. Knit 1-1/2 spools. If you are using the Magicord, use only one weight or less. The resulting cording will be very ″open″ in appearance, but this changes as the cording is used to make fringe or the hanging cord.

2. On the Tassel Master, place a row of pegs along Position #1 and a second row along Position #5.

3. Make two 10″ lengths of bullion fringe across the full Tassel Master board or four lengths across the Tatool, following instructions that come with the tool. Tape and remove from the board or tool.

4. Make another 5″ length of bullion fringe.

Making the Triple Bullion Hanging Cord

1. Make the first cord using two 1-1/2 yard lengths of the first perle #5 color held together with the ends knotted to form a circle. Hang the looped end over a hook and twist tightly. Hold the twisted cord with tape or a weight while you twist the second cord.

2. Make the second cord as the first but use two 1-1/2 yard lengths of the second perle #5 color held together as above and hold.

3. Make the third cord as the first, but use the 1/2 yard length of knitted cording. Do not remove from the twisting tool.

4. Insert the first twisted thread group into the twisting tool and reverse twist to create the double bullion cord.

5. Knot the ends together to create a circle, then double the cord.

Assembling the Tassel

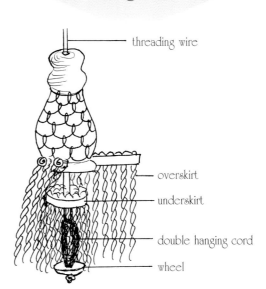

threading wire

overskirt

underskirt

double hanging cord

wheel

1. Insert the doubled cord into the threading wire and thread on the wheel, sliding it to the knot at the end.

2. Remove all but 1″ of the paper from the tape on the long length of the bullion fringe underskirt.

3. Starting at the paper-covered end, wrap the underskirt around the threading wire and insert the threading wire into the bottom of the finial.

4. Draw the hanging cord up, pulling the underskirt into the bottom of the finial, taking care not to catch in the bullion skirt.

5. Remove the paper cover from the remaining 5″ length of bullion fringe and wrap it around the lower neck of the tassel finial, tape side in.

6. Apply a dot of fabric glue on the back of each of the mini-roses and glue evenly spaced around the top of the overskirt.

Gemstone

The colors in this tassel remind me of emerald, lapis, turquoise, and amethyst, hence its name. This is another quite easy tassel to make and utilizes some very basic techniques embellished with beads.

Difficulty rating:
Beginner to Intermediate

Finished length
(excluding hanging cord):
7″

Materials & Tools

⚜ 2 large-hole wood beads, 3/4″ diameter and 1/8″ diameter
⚜ 1-1/2″ diameter wood bowl with 1/4″ hole drilled through center
  Note: Or use a 3″ long finial instead of the beads and bowl
⚜ 1″ wood wheel with 1/4″ center hole
⚜ 2 spools Multi's Embellishment Yarn, color Gemstone
⚜ 1 yd. teal chenille yarn
⚜ 1 spool purple rayon cord (heavy sewing thread)

⚜ 49 clear turquoise glass beads, 3mm
⚜ 4 turquoise glass beads in varying shapes, 6-9mm
⚜ double-faced tape, 1/4″ wide
⚜ fabric glue
⚜ dental floss threader or beading needle
⚜ threading wire
⚜ twisting tool (Spinster, Custom Corder, or pencil)
⚜ Magicord Machine or spool knitter
⚜ Tassel Master or Tatool

Making the Finial

1. Glue the three wood parts together, making sure the holes line up vertically. Let dry. This is now the finial.

2. Spray the finial with adhesive and let set.

3. Cut three 4-yard lengths of Multi's and knot each of the ends together to form three separate circles. Hang the looped end over a hook and twist. Bring the knotted end to the looped end and let the yarn double back on itself to create the bullion cording. Knot the ends to secure. Repeat for the other two circles of Multi's.

4. Wrap the top bead with the Multi's bullion cording. Wrap the center bead with chenille, and the bowl with Multi's bullion cording.

5. Cut a 10″ length of Multi's and thread it with 17 3mm turquoise beads. Knot the end. Tie this around the finial between the top and center wood beads (so there is a row of beads around the finial). Apply a dot of glue to the knot and snip off the excess yarn.

6. Cut a 12″ length of Multi's and thread on 25 3mm beads. Knot the end securely and apply a dot of glue to the knot. Tie the Multi's around the lower part of the finial so the beads encircle the finial between the lower bead and the wood bowl. Let the ends of the Multi's hang down.

7. Thread one hanging length of Multi's with three 3mm beads, two of the larger glass beads, and one 3mm bead.

8. Slide the beads toward the finial and cut the yarn to measure 5″. Make a knot in the end of the yarn, place a drop of glue on the knot, let set, and let the beads drop to the knot. Snip off the excess yarn.

9. On the remaining length of hanging yarn, thread on one 3mm bead, two larger glass beads, and two 3mm beads. Slide the beads toward the finial, make a knot at the end of the yarn, apply a dot of glue to the knot, and snip off the excess.

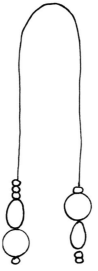

Making the Tassel Overskirt

1. Use the Magicord Machine or the spool knitter to knit one full spool Multi's into cording.

2. If using the Tassel Master, insert one row of pegs across Position #1 and a second row across Position #5. If using the Tatool, set it at 5″.

3. Twist the cording lightly as you wrap across one full length of the Tassel Master board or two lengths of the Tatool. Apply double-faced tape 1/8″ from the top, following instructions that come with the tool and remove the yarn from the board or tool.

Making the Tassel Underskirt

1. Make the cut-skirt fringe for the underskirt by wrapping one strand of rayon cord and one strand of Multi's around the Tassel Master pegs (full board length with pegs in Positions #1 and #5) or Tatool (two full frame lengths), following the manufacturer's instructions. Apply tape and remove from the tool.

Making the Single Bullion Hanging Cord

1. Cut three 1-yard lengths of Multi's and twist to create a single bullion cord. Knot the ends together to form a circle.

Assembling the Tassel

1. Thread the wheel onto the hanging cord and slide it to the knot.

2. Remove all but the first 1/2″ of paper from the tape.

3. Starting with the paper-covered end, wind the fringe around the threading wire.

4. Insert the threading wire into the base of the finial and pull up the hanging cord, pulling the skirt into the bottom of the finial.

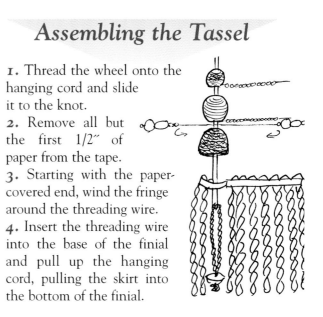

Autumn Elegance

This tassel is not only easy, but fun. The loftiness of the acrylic yarn used for the skirt gives just the right look for a toast to autumn. Add your own preferences in trim or colors and you have a whole new tassel design.

Difficulty rating:
Beginner

Finished length (including bead, excluding hanging cord):
10˝

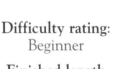

Materials & Tools

- 🎋 wood finial that comes with Tassel Master or 2-3/4˝ high finial with bored-out base and lower lip
- 🎋 100-yd. spool acrylic punch yarn in each the following colors: dark green, medium green, peach, rust, soft gold, toast
- 🎋 1/4 yd. gold braid, 5/8˝ wide
- 🎋 1/4 yd. soutache braid, 1/8˝ wide
- 🎋 1 skein cotton embroidery floss each of medium green and dark rust
- 🎋 dark brown wood bead, 1˝ diameter

- 🎋 willow green acrylic paint
- 🎋 paintbrush
- 🎋 matte glaze
- 🎋 double-faced tape, 1/4˝ wide
- 🎋 fabric glue
- 🎋 threading wire
- 🎋 twisting tool (Spinster, Custom Corder, or pencil)
- 🎋 small accordion peg rack or swift
- 🎋 5-peg spool (helpful but not required)

Making the Finial

1. Paint the finial and let dry.
2. Apply a coat of glaze and let dry.
3. Wrap the 5/8″ wide braid around the lower edge of the finial and glue in place.
4. Wrap the soutache braid over the braid just attached and glue in place.
5. Repeat Steps 3 and 4 for the middle "neck" of the finial.

Making the Tassel Skirt with a Peg Rack

1. Open the peg rack so the peg sets are 7″ apart.
2. Holding one of each of the colors of punch yarn together, cut off 10 yards and set aside.
3. Wind the rest of the yarn around one set of pegs.
4. Cut a 36″ length of floss and tie the tassel securely through all the thicknesses of yarn at the top of one of the pegs.
5. Open up the rack to release the tassel.
6. Cut through the loops at the lower edge.

Making the Tassel Skirt with a Swift

1. Open up the swift so there is a 42″ circumference measured when the yarn is wound around it.
2. Holding one of each of the colors of punch yarn together, cut off 10 yards and set aside.
3. Wind the rest of the yarn around the swift.
4. Cut three 12″ lengths of cotton floss and tie them around the yarn securely in three equally spaced lengths through all thicknesses of yarn.
5. Collapse the swift to release the tassel skirt.
6. Cut through all thicknesses of yarn between the ties.
7. Join all three sections of the skirt by tying securely around the center of all three.
8. Snip off the first three floss ties.

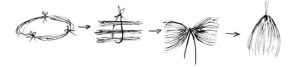

Making the Double Triple Bullion Hanging Cord

1. Cut four 36″ lengths of the group of punch yarns. Set two aside.
2. Make each into a circle.
3. Twist the first group and hold. Twist the second group and hold.
4. With the embroidery floss, cut two 36″ lengths and twist for the third bullion.
5. Hook all the twisted yarn onto one hook and reverse twist.
6. Repeat Steps 2 through 5.
7. Holding each length of cording together, twist lightly and make into a thick, double bullion cord.
8. Wrap the group of yarns together over the end of the cord and secure in the back with glue.

Assembling the Tassel

1. Insert the threading wire with the floss holding the tassel skirt.
2. Draw it through the finial.
3. Thread the bead onto the floss and tie the floss "into" the bottom end of the hanging cord. Apply a dot of glue to the knot and snip off the excess floss.

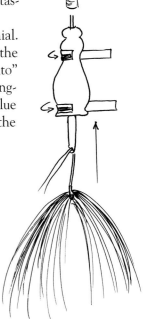

Wire-Wrapped Holiday Tassel

With wire crafting so popular, this tassel not only gives you an enjoyable way to work with wire-wrapping, but adds accent to any holiday décor. It also matches the tasseled centerpiece on page 116.

Difficulty rating:
Beginner

**Finished length
(excluding the hanging cord):**
5″

Materials & Tools

- ❋ plastic chair leg protector cap, 1″ diameter x 1-1/2″ high
- ❋ 1″ diameter metal washer
- ❋ rayon crochet thread or chainette, 1 ball burgundy, 1 ball dark green
- ❋ 1 spool 20mm gold wire
- ❋ 6 dark red beads of varying shapes
- ❋ 6 gold beads, 3mm
- ❋ spray adhesive
- ❋ fabric glue

- ❋ crochet fork, Tassel Master, or Tatool
- ❋ drill with 1/4″ bit
- ❋ sewing machine
- ❋ threading wire
- ❋ double-faced tape, 1/4″ wide
- ❋ needle-nose pliers
- ❋ round-nose pliers
- ❋ twisting tool (Spinster, Custom Corder, or pencil)

Making the Finial

1. Drill a hole in the bottom of the chair leg cap.
2. Apply a thick coat of spray adhesive and let set.
3. Starting at the top, wrap the cap with dark green crochet thread or chainette.
4. Thread all the beads on a 14″ length of wire and use the pliers to bend the wire as desired to fit easily around the finial. Arrange the beads randomly in a pleasing design (refer to the photo). Cut off the excess wire.

Making the Ruff

1. Position the metal bars of the crochet fork at 1″.
2. Measure the circumference of the lower edge of the finial (the ruff edge) and wind burgundy thread on the crochet fork for this measurement.
3. Using the zipper foot, sew along the upper edge of the wrapped thread. Remove from the frame.

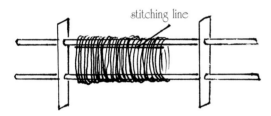

stitching line

4. Cut along the bottom edge.
5. Wrap the ruff around the lower edge of the finial and use glue or double-faced tape to secure it.
6. Wrap a piece of wire twice over the stitching line.

Making the Tassel Skirt

1. If using the Tassel Master, place a row of pegs along Position #1 and a second row along Position #5. If using the crochet fork or Tatool, set for 5″. Holding one strand of burgundy and one of green thread together, make a 10″ length (across the full Tassel Master board or crochet frame or two lengths of the Tatool).

2. Apply tape along the length, 1/8″ from the top.
3. Remove the fringe from the board or tool.

Making the Single Bullion Hanging Cord

1. Cut one yard each of the burgundy and green thread.
2. Hold the two strands together and knot to form a circle.
3. Twist to form a bullion cord. Tie the ends together and knot to form a circle.

Assembling the Tassel

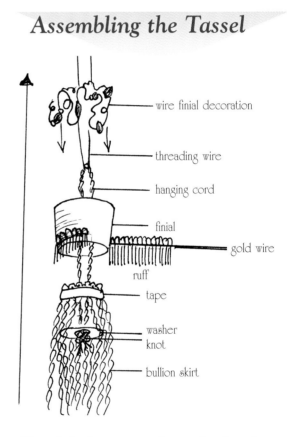

wire finial decoration
threading wire
hanging cord
finial
gold wire
ruff
tape
washer
knot
bullion skirt

1. Thread the hanging cord into the threading wire and thread on the washer. Then insert the threading wire into the bottom of the finial.
2. Remove all but 1″ of the paper covering the tape and wrap the tassel skirt around the threading wire, starting with the paper-covered end. Insert the wire into the bottom of the finial.
3. Draw the cord through, pulling the skirt into the bottom of the finial, taking care not to catch in the bullion skirt.

Holiday Candle Centerpiece

*C*ombining *the popular use of decorative wire with Christmas cheer, this center-piece can stand on its own, be put on a holder, or surrounded with an evergreen wreath for the perfect complement to a decorative table setting or occasional table accent.*

Difficulty rating:
Intermediate

**Finished length
of each tassel:**
3˝

Materials & Tools

❈ 6˝ diameter candle with multiple wicks
❈ 1 spool 18-20 gauge brass wire
❈ 6 plastic dowel or chair leg caps, 5/8˝diam-eter x 5/8˝ high
❈ chainette yarn or rayon cord: 1 spool dark green, 1 spool cranberry
❈ spray adhesive
❈ double-faced tape, 1/4˝ wide

❈ fabric glue
❈ awl
❈ round-nose pliers
❈ threading wire
❈ twisting tool (Spinster, Custom Corder, or pencil)
❈ Tassel Master or crochet fork

Making the Finial

1. Use the awl to punch a 1/8″ hole in the bottom of each chair cap.
2. Spray all of the caps with adhesive and let set.
3. Wrap three of the caps with dark green chainette and three with cranberry.

Making the Single Bullion Hanging Cord

1. Cut three 36″ lengths of dark green chainette and three of cranberry.
2. Working each length of chainette separately, fold the strand in half and loop the fold over a hook.
3. Knot the ends to form a circle and twist tightly.
4. Bring the ends together, letting the thread double back on itself to create the bullion cording.
5. Make a double knot by bringing the ends together to form a circle. Repeat to make six cords. Set aside. *Note:* The hanging cords should be no more than 1-1/4″ long, excluding the knot. If your cording is longer, make the knot higher on the cording and cut off the excess.

Making the Tassel Skirt

1. On the Tassel Master, place a row of pegs in Position #1 on the upper board and another row in Position #3. If using the crochet fork, position the bars 2-1/2″ apart.
2. Wrap one strand of cranberry and one strand of green chainette together around the board or frame until there is a 9″ length, making sure the threads don't overlap.
3. Apply double-faced tape across the top of the fringe and remove it from the board or frame.
4. Repeat Steps 1 through 3.
5. Cut each length of fringe into thirds for a total of six 3″ lengths.

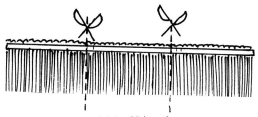

cut into 3″ lengths

6. Wrap one 3″ skirt section around one of the hanging cords just above the knot.
7. Insert the threading wire in the loop of the hanging cord and draw the tassel skirt into the bottom of the finial.

Making the Decorative Wire Wrap

1. Working each piece separately, bend three 24″ sections of wire in a scroll for hanging the tassels. There is no right or wrong way to bend the wire - it's all up to you. You can always cut off any excess wire.
2. To hold each of the three sections together, forming a circle around the candle, cut a joining wire and twist it in shape.
3. To hold the wire frame around and on the candle, make three "staples" by bending three pieces of wire into the shape of a staple. Then, on three points around the candle, push the wire ends into the candle. (Tip: Warming the ends of the "staples" helps pierce the candle.)

joining wire

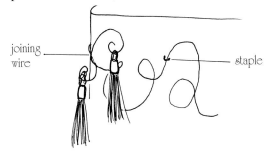

joining wire   staple

4. Hang the tassels on the scrolled ends of the wire.

Chapter IX

Meet the Experts

Suzann Thompson:
Master Designer of the Fiber
& Polymer Clay Marriage

Combining Techniques in a Tassel

by Suzann Thompson

Suzann Thompson.

How can a person combine a love for yarn, beads, polymer clay, crochet, and an inherited passion for bits of pretty china? In a tassel, of course! That's why I like them so much. After years of knitting, crocheting, making jewelry, and crafting in polymer clay, I've collected boxes and tubs and drawers full of supplies. In tassel making, I can use all my treasures together.

Tassels will probably always be used in home decorating, but for the future I see memory tassels and gift tassels. For memories of schooldays, use school colors in the tassel skirt and decorate with charms and letter beads. Work seashells into a tassel skirt to remind you of a vacation at the beach. Or if you have broken a favorite cup or plate, use the pieces for a mosaic tassel top, as I did in the China Blues Tassel pictured on page 119.

Metal charms and ornaments are available in a wide range of motifs, whether you love cats or hearts, cowboys or needlework (see Resources on page 128). A tassel decorated with musical instruments, clefs, and eighth-note charms would be a great gift for your favorite music lover. The same is true for miniatures. A knitting friend might enjoy a tassel with its skirt made of knitting yarns and the finial decorated with a miniature knitting basket, *How to Knit* book, and tiny scissors. Look for miniatures at a dollhouse store or check the miniatures section of a craft store. Seed-bead tassels make great jewelry. Hang them from a stick-pin, earring wires, or a short necklace. I've even seen tiny tassels hanging from the back seam of some lovely high heels. The effect was sophisticated but very playful.

However you decide to use your tassels, have fun making them. No tassel police will issue citations for "Violations of Section 3.4: Outlandish Tassel Making," so give your imagination free rein. The four tassels pictured are samples of how you can use unconventional materials and your imagination to create unique works of art.

China Blues Tassel. *The form for the China Blues tassel was an eggshell broken out after baking. I covered the base layer with a second layer of clay, then glued and pressed the china shards into this layer and baked. I filled the spaces between the china pieces with sausages of gold-colored clay, smoothed them carefully, and baked again. One of the strands in the skirt is crocheted. I threaded beads onto gold lamé thread, then chained, with a bead in every seventh stitch.*

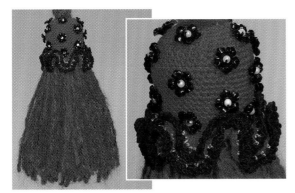

Spanish Dancer Tassel. *The Spanish Dancer tassel has a crocheted top. I crocheted the skirt together in a spiral fashion, then kept single crocheting around and around, increasing and decreasing to make the top. I inserted a straw and stuffed the top tightly with polyester stuffing. I crocheted a second top, which fits over the first. The ruffle is made by working three double crochet stitches into the front loop of each stitch around the bottom of the finial, then another round of three double crochets into the back loop of each stitch. Each ruffle is trimmed with a round of gold and a round of black. The flower beads were sewn on, and I pulled the ends of the hanging cord through the straw and tied them under the skirt.*

Chandelier. *I made the long section of the skirt for Chandelier using the Tassel Master tool with its halves clamped on either end of a Black & Decker Work-Mate. The WorkMate clamps flat objects from side-to-side (as opposed to c-clamps, which clamp from top-to-bottom). I moved the Tassel Master halves together for the medium strands. The short section is made on the Tassel Master's longest setting, but I still clamped it for stability. Use weights, like canned vegetables or boxed fruit juice, to hold the strands on the combs or pegs. The top, worked over a foil-covered drinking glass is a layer of Premo Sculpey Pearl with pre-baked bits pressed into it. After baking, I sanded the surface. The trim is made of sausages of clay glued around the edges and then baked.*

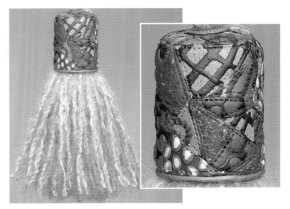

Pink Patchwork Tassel. *In this tassel I combined my interest in quilting and sewing with tassel-making. I used a 35mm film canister as a mold and rolled sheets of five different colors of clay, then decorated each one differently. These formed the 'fabrics' used in the patchwork. The stitching lines were made with a tracing wheel from my sewing box. Cutting slices of various combinations of colors then cutting them into a patchwork and applying them to the mold was just half the fun. Creating the mock-stitching lines and adding the fluffy mohair blend skirt was the other half. (For detailed instructions on the techniques used to make the Pink Patchwork Tassel, please see Suzann's book* The Polymer Clay Sourcebook *(Hamlyn, 1999).*

Using Polymer Clay

Polymer clay is a wonderful medium for beginners and experts alike. It is a plastic compound that is permanently cured by baking it in your home oven. It comes in many colors or you can blend your own. Most crafters probably already have everything they need to work with polymer clay, though people who work with it a lot usually invest in special tools. Here is an annotated list of basic tools and supplies you need for to make the Fantasy Flower tassel (page 121) and general polymer clay crafting.

<u>Work surface</u>: non-shiny ceramic tiles are best because you can bake your work on the tile, too. Other good surfaces are stone tiles, glass, or kitchen worktop laminate. Never work with clay or leave it on a varnished surface or on most hard plastics. The plasticizers in the clay can damage them.

<u>Oven</u>: for best results, test the baking temperature of your oven with an oven thermometer.

<u>Baking trays</u>: ceramic tiles are good. You can also use a cookie sheet lined with white copier paper. The paper won't burn and it will keep your pieces from developing a shiny spot where they touch the baking surface.

<u>Blades</u>: a craft knife is useful. I also recommend that you invest in a long, thin blade. Some are made specifically for polymer clay crafting (see Resources on page 128). Other blades work just as well: a wallpaper-scraper replacement blade from your hardware store or a tissue blade from a medical supply store. Be careful with these blades as they are very sharp.

<u>Rolling tools</u>: to make uniform, thin sheets of clay, use a print roller, a length of PVC pipe, or a smooth, cylindrical drinking glass (not plastic). I use a pasta machine to quickly make uniform sheets of clay. Once you use a pasta machine for polymer clay, never use it again for food preparation.

<u>Misc</u>: Keep some supplies on hand, like Super Glue and wet/dry sandpaper (grades 240, 400, 600, 1000).

Design Notes

You can't always walk down to the corner store and buy tassel-making supplies, particularly the finials. My challenge for the tassel I designed for this book was to make it without the traditional tassel finial. Polymer clay (best known by brand names FIMO, Premo, Sculpey, Cernit, and others) is my first choice, though I've experimented with crocheted and seed-beaded finials.

Polymer clay finials usually require some sort of form. Wrap a straight or flared glass or a film canister with aluminum foil to make it easy to slide out. Cover the form with a thin layer of scrap clay and make a 1/4″ diameter hole in the middle of the end. Bake and let cool. Fresh clay sticks fairly well to the baked scrap clay layer. Use a little Super Glue to stick stubborn pieces. Likewise, if you cover a form that will become part of the finished tassel, you can use Super Glue to hold the uncured clay decorations in place. Curvy forms, like traditional turned wooden tassel finials, will become part of the finished tassel because you can't slide them out of a clay covering.

Bake the uncovered finial for 20 minutes at about 250°F to dry out any moisture lurking inside. Then cover it with clay and bake it again. For a professionally smooth finish, sand the baked clay with wet/dry sandpaper in a large bowl of water or under a thin stream of running water. Begin with the coarsest grade and move to progressively finer grades. Buff with a terry towel for a subtle shine. For a very shiny finish, use a bench-mounted lathe fitted with a musliln buffing wheel. Barely touch the polymer clay to the spinning buffing wheel. If you accidentally buff ruts in the clay, sand to smooth and buff more gently next time.

Most of my tassel skirts are made using the Tassel Master tool with three or more strands of novelty knitting yarns twisted together. My tassel skirts are anchored in the finials with a polymer clay button. Roll a ball of clay and flatten it to about 1/4″ thick (you may have to experiment to find the amount of clay appropriate for the size of your tassel). Bore two holes in the flattened piece with a straw or a round clay cutter. Bake the button.

To finish the tassel, thread the taped hanging cord ends through the end of the finial and through the middle of the skirt. Thread one end through each hole in the button, push the button as far up into the skirt as you can, and tie the ends with a square knot.

Trim the ends and free any fringes that are caught up under the button. If you wish, put glue on the knot.

Fantasy Flower Tassel

This tassel is an elaboration of some very basic techniques used in combination with each other. The beads are an easy but dramatic accent to an otherwise relatively basic design.

Materials & Tools

- 1 package each of Sculpey SuperFlex in White and Yellow (this stays flexible even after curing)
- 1 package each of Premo! Sculpey in Zinc Yellow, Orange, Fuchsia, Fluorescent Pink, Sea Green, Green; scraps of Ultramarine Blue
- empty round (not oval) 35mm film canister, without the lid
- aluminum foil

- drinking glass or glass vase about 7″ tall
- sturdy cardboard, 4″ x 4″
- white paper
- masking tape
- yarn hanging cord
- garlic press (optional, not to be used for food preparation again)
- general supplies and equipment as described on page 120

Making the Tassel Skirt

1. Condition 1/2 package of Sculpey SuperFlex White. Divide the clay into two portions. Press one portion through the garlic press; do not cut the strands. Open the garlic press, insert the second portion, and press it through. Use a blade to slice the strands off the press. If you do not use a garlic press, roll the White clay into long cylinders about 1/8″ (3mm) in diameter, and cut two strands 7″ long, two strands 6-3/4″ long, two strands 6-1/2″ long, and so on, decreasing by 1/4″ for each set of strands until you reach approximately 2″. Aim for 35-40 strands.

2. Repeat Step 1 with the SuperFlex Yellow.

3. Arrange the strands from the shortest to the longest. Pick up the shortest White strand and the shortest Yellow strand. Twist them together to make a candy-cane twist. Roll the twist gently on your work surface to smooth it. Twist it more if desired. On one end, turn a tight spiral in the twist. These spirals are meant to be the ends of the stamens of the flower (refer to the photo). Repeat with all the strands, pairing White and Yellow strands of the same length.

4. Bake the twisted strands following the manufacturer's instructions and let cool. Arrange them from shortest to longest.

5. The rest of the tassel is made with Premo! Sculpey. Condition specific colors as needed. With Yellow, roll a cylinder about 3/8″ in diameter and 10″ long. Flatten the cylinder into a strip about 1/16″ thick. Place a sheet of white paper along the long edge of this strip.

6. Beginning about 1/4″ from one end of the strip, press the plain end of the shortest twist (from Step 2) into the strip, with the rest of the twist resting on the paper. Press the next longest twist into the strip, next to the previous twist, and repeat until all the twists are pressed into the strip.

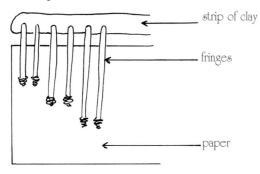

strip of clay

fringes

paper

7. Use a blade to loosen the strip from the work surface. Beginning at the end of the strip where the longest twist is, tightly roll up the paper *and* the clay strip. The paper should be separate from the clay strip, but should be right up against it. The paper protects the twists and keeps them separate during baking. Tape the end of the paper shut with a piece of masking tape. This is the tassel skirt.

8. Cut a hole in the middle of the cardboard just wide enough for the rolled tassel skirt and paper to fit through. Set this and the tassel skirt aside.

Making the Finial

1. Cover the film canister with a layer of foil. Roll the Orange clay to a layer 1/8″ thick and cover the bottom of the film canister and halfway up the side. Trim the edge neatly. Make a 3/8″ diameter hole in the center of the bottom of the canister, which will be the top of the tassel. Bake for 10 minutes and let cool. Remove the Orange cover from the canister. This is the core of the tassel finial.

2. Roll a long, thin layer of Orange. Patch and re-roll as necessary to create a strip 3/4″ wide x 4″ long (roll larger and trim to size). Repeat this procedure with Yellow. Place the Yellow strip on top of the Orange strip and roll this assembly out longer (not wider), until it is about 1/16″ thick.

3. Gather one long edge of the strip, Yellow side up, around the bottom edge of the Orange core, being careful that the ruffle formed on the other edge of the strip doesn't stick to itself. (You may wish to practice this first with a solid color of clay. You can remove and reuse the solid color.) Flare the ruffle around the outside, and flatten the gathered edge onto the Orange core. Trim the length if necessary and smooth the join as well as you can. Place this on a piece of paper and bake for 10 minutes. Let cool.

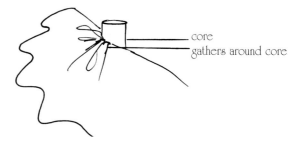

core

gathers around core

4. Repeat Step 2, only this time roll and trim the strips to 6˝ long. Repeat Step 3, pressing the gathered edge just above the previous ruffle. This ruffle will have more bends, because the strip is longer. Bake again for 10 minutes and let cool.

5. Roll a long, thin layer of Fluorescent Pink. Patch and re-roll as necessary to create a strip 1˝ wide x 6˝ long (roll larger and trim to size). Repeat this procedure with Fuchsia. Place the Fuchsia strip on top of the Fluorescent Pink strip and roll this assembly out longer, until it is about 1/16˝ thick.

6. Gather the strip as before, Fuchsia side up, just above the previous ruffle. Bake for 10 minutes and let cool.

7. Roll a 1/16˝ thick layer of Ultramarine Blue. Cut five narrow triangles about 1/4˝ wide at the base, and 1-1/4˝ tall. Twist them gently from the pointed end and press the bases of the triangles evenly spaced around the core, just above the last ruffle. They will rest on the ruffle. Bake for 10 minutes and let cool.

8. Repeat Step 2, only this time roll and trim the strips to 8˝ long. Gather the final strip around the top edge of the core. Bake 10 minutes and let cool.

9. Roll a 1/16˝ thick layer of Green. Cut a circle to cover the top of the core and the gathered edge of the last ruffle. (A circular petit fours 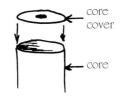 cutter works well or a ruffle-edged biscuit cutter, but don't use it for food again.) Cut a hole in the middle of the circle over the hole in the core.

10. Roll a thin layer of Green and trim to about 3/4˝ wide x several inches long. Repeat with Sea Green. Place the Sea Green on top of the Green. Make five leaves by folding and trimming this strip as shown in the illustration. Place the leaves evenly around the hole in the top of the finial, folded side up. Bake for 10 minutes and let cool.

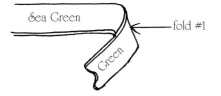

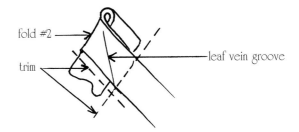

11. Make a sausage of Green clay about 3˝ long x 3/8˝ in diameter. Form it into a raindrop-shaped loop, pinch the ends together and taper them. Bake for 10 minutes.

Putting It Together

1. Squeeze and press the unbaked end of the tassel skirt inside the finial as far as you can. Leave the paper in place. Place a small ball of Green clay into the hole on top of the finial. Press the pointed end of the Green loop from Step 11 into the hole and into the ball of clay.

2. Thread the rolled tassel skirt through the hole in the cardboard (see Step 8 of Making the Tassel Skirt). The Yellow and Orange ruffle should rest on the cardboard. Hang the tassel inside the drinking glass or vase, with the cardboard resting on the rim. Bake 20 minutes and let cool.

3. Remove the tassel from the glass, take away the cardboard, and carefully remove the white paper from the tassel skirt. Tie a hanging cord around the loop.

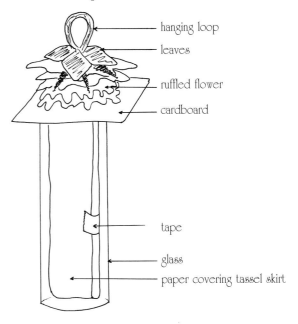

Alma Gulsby: Sewer, Teacher, Inventor

Alma Gulsby.

I "met" Alma when I ordered her E-Z Winder and spools from Clotilde's catalog. I thought they would be great as holders for twisted yarn to use on Tassel Master, but what I found was lots more than a great product. I met a very creative and dedicated woman who lives and breathes her product and her sewing/crafting lifestyle. I thought it would be great if the spools could be used to actually twist the yarns the way Alma used the bobbin winder of her sewing machine for winding the spools. So I e-mailed Alma, whose web address was listed on her product. Co-incidentally, she was in the process of designing just the tool I was hoping for! She sent me a few designs for the product to test on Tassel Master and the one she now produces is the one that worked the best. I must say, this tool makes tassel and fringe-making incredibly fast.

For those of you who may not be sewers but who may have an older sewing machine you use very little – you now have a reason to use it a lot!

Necessity Is the Mother of Invention

by Alma Gulsby

I developed the E-Z Twister/Winder because I wanted to learn decorative sewing on my serger. Number 30 crochet thread is the easiest thread to use while learning to master decorative serger stitches but it is not sold on spools and I had to spend more time hand winding it onto spools than I spent serging with it. Then I discovered all those beautiful threads and yarns for knitting and crocheting and I knew I had to solve the spool winding problem. Now I can quickly wind decorative thread to my heart's content using my machine bobbin winder and as an added bonus I can buy one cone of serger thread and wind as many additional spools as I need.

E-Z Twister/Winder.

I developed the E-Z Twister Spools after seeing a very pricey vest with beaded fringe in a New York department store. I wanted to make one but I didn't want to pay $30 a yard for fringe that wasn't even in the color I wanted. I also wanted bullion fringe but didn't want to twist the thread and yarn by hand. I needed a way to make lots of twisted thread and yarn and be able to keep it from doubling back on itself while I made the fringe. The solution was to modify one of my E-Z Twister/Winder spools and use the E-Z Twister/Winder and a sewing machine bobbin winder to twist the thread or yarn, then to use the same Twister/Winder to wind it onto the spool. It worked like a charm and all went well until I got to the task of forming the fringe. I used a crochet fork and it worked well enough, but it took a long time before I figured out how to do it without using three hands. Tassel Master makes it much easier and faster to make fringe and tassels, plus bullion length is much more consistent.

Alma's Amulet Purse

Making the Purse & Cord

Note: Use 1/2″ seam allowances.

1. Cut 80″ lengths of the following: two lengths of Multi's and one length of rose pink metallic floss and one strand of light pink perle #5. Make one 36″ length of bullion cording by holding all strands together and joining to make a circle. Hang the looped end over a hook and twist. Bring the knotted end to the looped end and let the yarn double back on itself to create the bullion cording. Knot the ends to secure and set aside.

2. Fuse the interfacing to the wrong side of the fabric. (If you plan to add the optional initial, do it now, using two strands of Multi's and one strand of metallic floss held together. Draw the initial in the desired location, then create a 6″ length of bullion cording using two strands of Multi's and three strands of a 6-strand length of metallic floss held together. Follow the instructions in step 1. Using fabric glue or fabric basting glue, affix the cording to form the initial. Zigzag stitch with matching thread.)

3. Fold the fabric in half, right sides together. From the folded end, measure down 3″ and mark.

4. Sew along both sides from the fold to the mark, backstitching at the beginning and end of

Materials & Tools

- 6″ x 27″ piece of pink moire fabric
- 6″ x 27″ piece of medium weight fusible interfacing
- 3/4″ shank button
- 3 spools Sunrise color Multi's Embellishment Thread
- 1 skein light pink perle #5 cotton yarn
- 1 skein 6-strand rose pink metallic embroidery floss
- masking tape
- fabric glue
- E-Z Twister
- Tassel Master

the seam. (This is the flap that folds over and closes the purse.)

5. Fold back the unsewn ends and press a 1/2″ hem to the wrong side on one end.

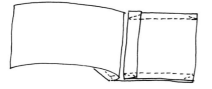

6. On the other end, press a 3/4″ hem to the wrong side. With right sides together, bring the hem end up to the end of the stitching at the 3″ mark and sew from the outer edge of the hem using a 1/2″ seam allowance and graduating to a 3/4″ seam allowance at the fold (this is the purse lining).

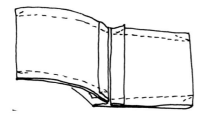

7. Trim the seam allowance to 1/4″ and finger press all the seams open.

8. Turn the closing flap and body of the purse right side out. Don't turn the lining.

9. Sew the button to the body of the purse just below the point of the purse flap.

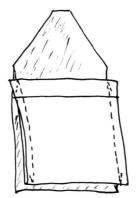

10. Slip the lining into the body of the purse and slip stitch the lining to the purse.

11. Knot the ends of the cording together to form a knot. Measure 2″ above the knot and with matching thread, use an overcast stitch to sew the bullion cord around the edges of the purse flap. (If you are careful, the thread will fall into the groove of the bullion cord, making it almost invisible.) Or use a cording foot and sew it by machine using a zigzag stitch.

12. Leave the remaining cording loose for the shoulder/neck strap.

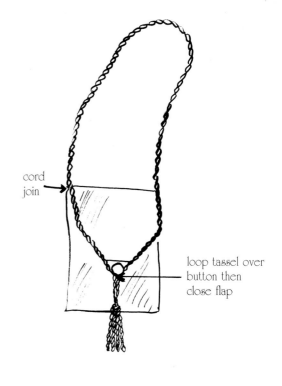

cord join

loop tassel over button then close flap

Making the Tassel

1. Using the E-Z Twister/Winder and holding one strand of Multi's and one strand of 6-strand metallic floss together, twist tightly and wind enough twisted yarn to fill the spool 3/4 full.

2. Insert one row of pegs along Position #2 and one row along Position #3 on the Tassel Master.

3. Wind the twisted yarn around the pegs for the length of the Tassel Master board and tape along the top.

4. Release the twisted yarn to create the bullion fringe and remove it from the board.

5. Stitch along the top to secure. Remove the tape.

6. Cut one 12″ strand each of Multi's and 6-strand metallic floss. Knot the ends to form a circle. Twist tightly to create bullion cording. Knot the ends together to form a circle.

7. Wrap the fringe just above the knot on the bullion cording and use fabric glue to secure.

8. Loop the cording with the tassel attached over the button before slipping the button through the cording attached to the purse flap.

About the Author

ari Clement is the president of CC Product Co./Bond America, manufacturer of the Incredible Sweater Machine (formerly the Bond machine) and other needlework tools. In 1999, she invented the Tassel Master after seeing how many tassels were being sold in stores at extremely high prices. Tassel Master allows anyone to make expensive-looking tassels and fringe from any type of yarn.

While writing this book, Cari enjoyed the challenge of designing tassels that use "found objects" for the finials and decorations, things like deodorant caps, taper candle decorations, nosegay bases, and many more. Not only are these tassel components easy to use, but they're very inexpensive and give a truly individual flavor to any project.

Cari's true joy is spending time with her daughter, Naima, who lives in New York City. Naima has taken up hand and machine knitting, sewing, mosaics, and sculpture. "There is nothing more enjoyable and rewarding than passing on years of information to one's kids and watching how they interpret that information into projects that reflect their own tastes," Cari says.

Cari presently lives in the Adirondack Mountains where she has the space for a complete studio. Her company is located in Glens Falls, New York, where she is working on a new design for the Sweater Machine.

Resources

3M Do-It-Yourself Division
Box 33053
St. Paul, MN 55133
800-934-7355
removable masking (drafting) tape

Access Commodities, Inc.
PO Box 1355
Terrell, TX 75160
972-563-3313
fancy yarns and threads

Aldastar
Division of DSR Mfg. Co.
70 Spruce St., 4th Floor, Bldg. 8
Paterson, NJ 07501
973-742-6787
PomBeadz

American Art Clay Co.
4717 W. 166th St.
Indianapolis, IN 46222
317-244-6871
www.amaco.com
polymer clay

Artemis
179 High St.
So. Portland, ME 04106
888-233-5187
artemis@ime.net
fancy silk ribbons

Artistic Wire Co.
1210 Harrison Ave.
LaGrange Park, IL 60526
630-530-7567
artwire97@aol.com
decorative wire

Beacon Adhesives
125 Macquesten Pkwy S
Mt. Vernon, NY 10550
914-699-3400
www.beacon1.com
Fabri-Tac glue

Beadbox, Inc.
1290 N. Scottsdale Rd.
Tempe, AZ 85281-1703
800-beadbox
www.beadbox.com
pearl drop beads

Berroco, Inc.
14 Elmdale Rd., Box 367
Uxbridge, MA 01569
508-278-2527
www.berroco.com
fancy yarns

Bond America
71 Lawrence St.
Glens Falls, NY 12801
800-862-5348
bond@netheaven.com
Tassel Master, Multi's Embellishment Yarn, finials and tassel tops, double-sided tape, Tapestry Tool Punch Needle Embroidery Kits

Clover Needlecraft, Inc.
1007 E. Dominguez St. Ste. L
Carson, CA 90746-3620
310-516-7846
Pompom Maker

Coats & Clark
Two Lakepointe Plaza, 4135
South Stream Blvd.
Charlotte, NC 28217
704-320-5800
www.coatsandclark.com
Trim Tool, acrylic crochet yarn

Creative Beginnings
PO Box 1330
Morro Bay, CA 93443
800-367-1739
www.creative-beginnings.com
brass charms and ornaments

Darr, Inc.
2370-G Hillcrest Rd. #121
Mobile, AL 36695-3838
www.darrsewnotions.com
E-Z Twister/Winder

DMC Corp.
South Hackensack Ave.
Port Kearny, Bldg. 10A
South Kearny, NJ 07032
973-589-0606
www.dmc-us.com
cotton, rayon, metallic floss and threads

Edmar Co.
4811 Calle Alto
Camarillo, CA 93012
805-484-2306
www.edmar-co.com
fancy rayon yarns and threads

Erdal Yarns Ltd.
303 5th Ave., Ste. 1104
New York, NY 10016
800-237-6594
fancy yarns: rayons, blends, chainette, chenille, gimp

Fire Mountain Gems
jade beads
third hand/third arm tool

Hollywood Trims
Division of Prym Dritz
PO Box 5028
Spartanburg, SC 29304
864-576-5050
www.dritz.com
polymer clay paintable finials

Kiti
300 N. Seminary Ave.
Woodstock, IL 60098-0368
815-338-7970
kitiinc@aol.com
lamp frames

Kreinik Manufacturing
3106 Timanus Ln., Ste. 101
Baltimore, MD 21244
410-281-0040
www.kreinik.com
fancy metallic yarns and threads, silk yarns

Lacis
3163 Adeline St.
Berkeley, CA 94703
www.lacis.com
Leonardo Rope Maker and other tools, wood and other finials

National Braid Mfg. Corp.
48-34 Van Dam St.
Long Island City, NY 11101
718-392-0216
chainette

On the Surface
PO Box 8026
Wilmette, IL 60091
847-256-7446
Tatool, fancy yarns

Polyform Products
1901 Estes Ave.
Elk Grove Village, IL 60007
847-427-0020
www.sculpey.com
Premo! Sculpey, Sculpey SuperFlex

Prairie Craft Company
346 Brittany Drive
PO Box 209
Florissant, CO 80816-0209
800-779-0615
blades and other polymer clay supplies

Qualin International Inc.
PO Box 31145
San Francisco, CA 94131-0145
415-333-8500
qualinint@aol.com
silk yarns

Rainbow Gallery
7412 Fulton Ave., #5
N. Hollywood, CA 91605
818-982-4496
fancy yarns and threads

Renaissance Ribbons
PO Box 699
Oregon House, CA 95962
916-692-0842
www.ribbons.com
fancy ribbons

Rhode Island Textile Co.
211 Columbus Ave.
PO Box 999
Pawtucket, RI 02862
401-722-3700
www.ritextile.com
fancy yarns and floss

Ruby Mills
Division of Elmore-Pisgah Co.
PO Box 311
Rutherfordton, NC 28139
800-633-7829
www.elmore-pisgah.com
fancy yarns: rayon chenille, matte and crochet yarns

Sea Glass, Inc.
150 St. Charles St.
Newark, NJ 07105
973-344-2222
Sea Glass

Sulky of America
3113-D Broadpoint Dr.
Harbor Heights, FL 33983
941-629-3199
www.sulky.com
fancy threads and chainette

Sullivan's
5521 Thatcher Rd.
Downers Grove, IL 60515
630-435-1530
wood finials

Therm O Web
770 Glenn Ave.
Wheeling, IL 60090
847-520-5200
www.thermoweb.com
double-sided tape

Wm. E. Wright Ltd. Partnership
85 South St.
PO Box 398
West Warren, MA 01092
800-628-9362
Boye crochet fork

YLI Corp.
161 West Main St.
Rock Hill, NC 29730
803-95-3100
ylicorp@rhtc.net
fancy threads and cords